Contents

Acknowledgements

First among my acknowledgements I have to thank my late (that is my deceased) workmates of yesteryear, those Ragged Trousered Philanthropists (as Mr Robert Tressell, in his book of that name, succinctly described them), who worked in the port transport industry for most of their lives, after having spent their best years in His Majesty's Armed Forces, fighting His Majesty's enemies. To them and their memory I take my hat off, more especially Terry, whose wide knowledge on so many subjects was a wonder to behold.

Second in line are of course, Smoky Joe's ladies, that is Rosie and the other one who served at the café's bar, Mrs Sweet and Miss Bitter. Between them their distinctive brands of verbicide, verbosity and body language was to me a treasure house of contradictions; their own personalities and foibles when dealing with Smoky Joe's Café's customers fascinated me beyond logical explanation.

Next I have to say how grateful I am for the continuous attention given to my writing by literary friends: Mrs Christine Morad; Mrs Denise Leppard; and Mr Philip Connolly; most especially Philip for his tutorage in the use of electronic gadgetry.

I must mention here too my tutor, the late professor Keith Thurley of the London School of Economics and Political Science, where I studied Personnel Management under his guidance, while on release from the London Dock Labour Board; and also the South West London College, where I attended a Work Study Practitioners Course under the auspices of the National Ports Council for the Port Transport Industry.

Finally to my wife Iris, for all the lonely hours she has spent while I have been writing and researching this tale of slaves, surfs and wage slaves.

Henry T. Bradford

Introduction

*T*his tale about slaves, serfs and wage slaves is based on a series of short lectures by Terry, a docker workmate with a university degree in history (and, judging by the extent of his wide knowledge on so many subjects, quite possibly other academic disciplines too, though I could not substantiate that), while he was working down a ship's hold, resting in Smoky Joe's café after finishing work in the evenings, and in a public house known throughout the docks as the bottom canteen.

The lectures on slavery, serfdom and wage slavery were begun after George, our ship's gang's down-hold foreman, attempted to castigate Terry for being away too long, together with Brains, the gang's tea boy, when they had gone off to collect the gang's tea box from the Port of London Authority's offices, which were situated between the Southern Docks quays and the river Thames. The ship's gang had begun to load bags of hot cement dust, which had only recently been bagged up straight from the cement works kilns, into the lower hold of a (black-funnelled and -hulled) Pacific & Orient line cargo ship.

Of course, one's memory tends to fade with the passing of the years, more especially as it relates to minor details, so I have had to refer to a number of text books. These are in keeping with the time under discussion, the mid-1950s, and include the following:

A Portrait of Britain 1485–1688, Mary R. Price and C.E.R.
     Mather (Clarendon Press, 1951)
English History, Britannic Home University Press, 13th
     edition
Chambers Encyclopaedia
How Much Do You Know, ed. Harold Wheeler (Odhams, no
     date)
The Future of Education, Sir Richard Livingstone
     (Cambridge University Press, 1941)
The Great Dock Strike, ed. Terry McCarthy (Weidenfeld and
     Nicholson, 1988)

Financial Times, 31 December 2006; 'Britain repays last of Allied war loans'

What the Butler Saw: Two Hundred Years of the Servant Problem, E.S. Turner (Michael Joseph, 1961)

The Great Encyclopaedia of Universal Knowledge (Odhams, no date)

Webster's Encyclopaedia, Chancellor Press Ltd

Work, Study and Related Management Services, Dennis A. Whitmore (Heinemann, 1968)

These then are the books from which Terry's tale of slaves, serfs, wage and wage slaves is authenticated. The story also includes the modern version of entrapment to work – enslavement for debt: a system first practised in Mexico and some American states, but now universal under the name of bank loans or mortgages. The name given to an individual debtor is a 'peon'; the system itself is known as peonage.

I hope the reader will be as intrigued as I am by the historic content of Terry's tale and by the social and economic facts that relate to the subject matter under discussion. I am particularly appalled by the way in which some classes, and even nations, subjugate and ill-treat their fellows. For example, in Mother Russia under the Czars (long before Joseph Stalin came on the political scene) the 'upper classes' abused the 'peasantry' in a tyrannical manner. This is clearly illustrated by Count Leo Nikolaievich Tolstoy (1828–1910) in his *The Hanging Czar: An Indictment of the Russian Government*, which was published by the Independent Labour Party in London, translated by C. and A. Maude: 'I take today's paper. Today the 9th May, the paper contains these words: "Today in Kherson on the Strelbitzky Field twelve not twenty peasants were hanged for an (alleged) attack made with intent to rob, on a landed proprietor's estate in the Elizabetgrad district."'

However, Tolstoy did not go on to explain whether the attack was a violent crime of assault or just a simple case of poaching the landowner's game or stealing his vegetables. One might suppose that the crime would have been treated in much the same manner in England or Wales at a magistrates or an assize court: the saying of the day among villagers was, 'It's as well to be hanged for [stealing] a sheep as a lamb.' Men, women and children could be executed for any one of up to 250 petty crimes, before a parliamentary review in 1861 finally reduced that number to just three; and you could be transported for life for poaching a rabbit, but not for stealing a coney – which is rather curious, don't you think?

There are three major points relating to this story that are not covered by Terry's lectures. First, in his book *Work, Study & Management Services*, Dennis A. Whitmore states under the heading 'Historical Growth', 'In common with most techniques used in management, the majority of those used in management services have no definite origins. The building of the Pyramids was apparently highly organised, and method study and non financial incentives were almost certainly used.' (No doubt Moses and the Israelites, had they still been around, could have elucidated this for him.)

Second, regarding slave trading. It must not be assumed that it was only Negroes who were forced into slavery by organised slave traders. The Egyptians, Greeks, Romans and Chinese were noted for their slave markets. And as for our own islands, it is documented that even up till the seventeenth century slavers came from North Africa into the Irish Sea to kidnap Welsh, Irish and English people whom they forced into slavery. Little was ever done to combat these slave poachers till Oliver Cromwell, the Lord Protector of the Commonwealth, promoted one of his Parliamentary Army colonels, one Robert Blake (1599–1657), to become his General at Sea. The English fleet, under Blake's command, defeated and drove away Prince Rupert's Royalist fleet, defeated Dutch fleets under Von Trump, De Ruyter and De Witt, and without doubt his greatest victory was the annihilation of the Spanish fleet in Santa Cruz Bay, which is said to have been 'one of the fiercest actions ever fought on land or at sea'. But as far as the British islanders were concerned, Blake's greatest contribution was the destruction of Turkish pirates and slave traders: his fleet sailed under the guns of Tunis into the harbour, and his sailors set fire to the pirate and slave-trading ships.

Third, one thing that surprises me most about the descendants of former Negro slaves is why those who wish to be repatriated have not demanded of subsequent American and British governments that they should be returned to Africa, with a first-class air or sea ticket. Yes, why haven't they? I'm sure I damn well would.

The Match That Ignited A Lecture On Slavery

*H*aving finished discharging a cargo of maggoty, flesh- and gristle-covered bones (imports from Asian countries that included India and Bangladesh, and quite possibly the North African territories of Egypt, Libya and Aden), from a ship berthed alongside Tilbury Docks Riverside Jetty, and having taken the obligatory day off for having worked a 'short night' (from 8 a.m. till midnight), our ship's gang met again in the Dock Labour Board Compound for the 7.45 a.m. call on. Here we found Charlie, our ship worker, waiting to pick us up for a Pacific & Orient Line cargo vessel that was berthed at 31 transit shed, Tilbury Docks, ready to load cement, heavy vehicles, motor cars and general cargo for several Far Eastern ports.

The job was unusual only insofar as P&O general cargo ships loaded exported cargoes in the Royal Albert Docks, so our gang members were very suspicious about P&O's motive for bringing this ship down river into Tilbury Docks, especially as we had been caught out by the 'maggoty bones' job at Tilbury Riverside Cargo Jetty only two days before. That ship too had been a diverted cargo ship. Neither of them had been shown in *Lloyd's List* of shipping as having been destined for discharging or loading cargoes in Tilbury

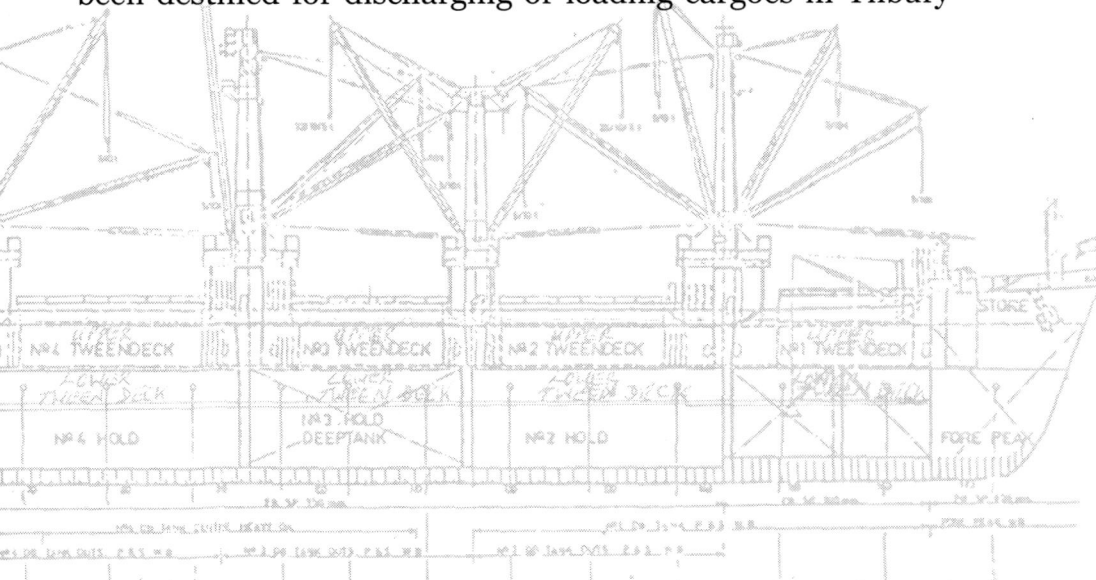

Docks. We were very suspicious.

However, Charlie our ship worker explained to us that all the Albert Dock berths were double banked with ships (one ship lying alongside another) and this particular one had been given priority because the bulk of her cargo was in Thames lighters, or Thames sailing barges, which were either already in Tilbury Docks, in the locks ready to enter Tilbury Docks, or on the way up the river Thames. Freight that was being delivered to the ship by road had also been diverted to Tilbury, and as most of it was heavy vehicles from British Leyland in the Midlands, motor cars from Ford of Dagenham, and light cargo for topping up purposes and beam filling from various other exporting merchants, there was no real urgency to strike the freight from road transport and railway wagons into the transit shed.

The cement that was to be stowed in the ship's lower holds and 'tween decks, had been brought from a cement manufacturer based beside the River Medway, in Thames sailing barges.

When I climbed up into the Stothard and Pitt quay crane cabin and looked down river, I could see the red barge sails of the sailing craft tacking back and forth across Gravesend Reach, their skippers using both wind and tide to keep their appointment with the black P&O cargo boat into which the barges would disgorge their cement. (When I think about it now, the whole operation was similar to watching sea birds regurgitate food into the mouths of their young.) There were also Thames lighters being drawn up river by a steam tug owned by Blue Circle Industries, the manufacturer of the lighters' cement freight. The lighters had set off from Cliffe Cement Works earlier in the morning, so as to catch the incoming tide. It was a convoy of dirty grey floating steel containers, each of which held between 80 and 120 tons of cement.

Cliffe Cement Works was several miles down river from Tilbury Docks, situated on the south bank of the Thames. It had its own deep water-loading jetty close to the ruins of Cliffe Fort. The cement was packaged in paper bags weighing one hundredweight each (fifty kilograms). The cement was still hot, as it had been bagged up straight out of the kilns. I had purposely asked the lighter-man to remove the hatches and had taken the beams off the cement carrying craft before removing the ship's slab hatches and beams, so that the heat from the bags of hot cement could escape into the atmosphere, to make the handling of it more comfortable for the barge hands.

While the barge hands were helping the lighter-man to remove his the hatches, the ship's down-holders had been busy clearing the deck on which they would land the ship's hatches and beams. Terry and Brains had decamped to the Tilbury Riverside Cargo Jetty to collect the gang's tea-box. It had taken them some time to find the Port Authority's jetty foreman, Mr Dunlop, who had kindly locked the tea-box in his office for safe keeping. So by the time Terry and Brains had returned to the ship, scrambled up the gangway carrying the tea-box between them, then climbed down through the deck hatch into the upper 'tween deck, the ship's gang had already began loading the hundredweight bags of cement into the ship's hold.

'What have you two lazy devils been doing?' George, the down-hold foreman, shouted up to them. 'It shouldn't have taken you all this time to collect our tea-box. It's damn near "Beer Ho", you two. It's about time you got back here to do some work. What do you think we are? Your soddin' slaves?'

This last remark brought not a few disgruntled remarks from the other down-holders, who were hurrying back and forth between the landing beds and the stowage in the lower hold with hundredweight bags of hot cement dust.

'Give over, George,' replied Terry, 'we've been trying to find the jetty foreman. He's as elusive as the Scarlet Pimpernel when there's no ships on the jetty. He'd locked the tea-box in his office.'

'Where is it now?'

'Up in the 'tween deck.'

'Brains,' said George, 'go and make a pot of tea. Terry, you come down here and start work, you lazy tea-swilling sot.'

As Brains climbed up through the deck hatch to retrieve the teapot from the gang's tea-box, and make his way to the ship's galley to scrounge hot water to make the tea, Terry lowered himself through the upper 'tween deck hatch, into the lower 'tween deck, on his way down into the lower hold, singing:

> I'm a little wage slave, loading bags of cement,
> Hot and heavy sacks of my employer's low paid torment,
> I load three hundred tons each day; it's just enough to pay my rent.
> Now if my rent is not paid, the bailiffs will come to my retreat,
> And throw my wife, my children and me out onto a cold bleak street.
> Yes, I'm a little wage slave, slaving all the day,
> Growing grey and getting older, on a wage slave's pay,
> And when I'm old and past wage slaving, I'll get my reward,
> I'll be dumped in a cold bleak workhouse, with a hard bed and part board,
> Then when I kick the bucket, like all us wage slaves finally do,
> Some magnanimous workhouse beadle will have me buried too:
> In a shallow unmarked pauper's grave, George, right next door to you.

'Cut out that cackling, Terry,' George shouted up at him, 'you'll be out of breath before you start work. There's 1,500 tons of cement to come down this hold, and you've not touched a single bag of it yet.'

'Beer Ho,' Brains called down the hold, just as Terry reached the bottom of the lower deck ladder. George turned away from the set of cement he was stowing and glared at Terry. Terry laughed and ran back up the lower hold ladder, as though the ship was sinking, with George in close pursuit, shouting, 'If I lay my hands on you, you lazy sot, I'll break both your arms.'

Terry, having reached the upper 'tween deck, scrambled through the deck hatch and waited. Then, as George's head emerged, Terry grabbed him playfully round his neck and said, 'You've got to get out of this arm lock first.'

'Let go, you stupid oaf,' said George, 'the tea will be getting cold.'

*****

The down-holders were sitting on the upper 'tween deck hatch covers, which they had rigged up as a table and seats, drinking their tea and eating their rolls or sandwiches, by the time the barge hands arrived on the scene. Terry had, as usual, separated from the rest of the gang; he was sitting on a piece of wood protruding from a stringer board, reading the *Daily Worker*. Charlie, one of the barge hands, shouted across the hatch to him, 'Does that Communist propaganda rag you're reading give the loading price for cement, Terry?'

'No,' replied Terry, without looking up from his newspaper, 'but the Port of London, Ocean Trades Piece-Work Rates price book does.'

'Have you got a loading price book?'

'Yes, I have. You can purchase one from the Union Office for sixteen pence.'

'Don't be such a mean sod. Look up the loading price of cement for me.'

'I could, but why do you want to know?'

'I'm trying to work out what our "tick note" will be if we can manage to load 300 tons of cement a day.'

Terry took his price book from his pocket, looked up cement, then shouted back to Charlie, 'Cement – paper bags – ship loading from craft – twelve men under quay crane – rate per ton four shillings and four pence.'

'How much does that work out each per ton?'

'Do the sum yourself,' said Terry.

'How?' replied Charlie.

'Holy Christ,' said Terry, 'there's twelve pence in one shilling, therefore multiply four shillings by twelve pence, that equals forty-eight pence, then you add the other four pence and you've got fifty-two pence; divide fifty-two by twelve and that gives you four pence three farthings per man per ton.'

'What does that work out per man if we do 300 tons a day?'

'Sweating bodies, fatigue, backache, and in retirement arthritis and bronchitis if we should live that long.'

'No, in wages, you idiot.'

'Well,' said Terry, '300 times four pence three farthings equals 1,425 pence; divide that by twelve, and that should give you 118 shillings and nine pence. Twenty shillings to the pound gives you five pounds, eighteen shillings and nine pence – or as near as damn it.'

'Cut that scheming out, Terry,' George shouted across the hold to him. 'If your tea's too hot, throw it away and get back down the lower hold. You bloody communists, they should ship the lot of you over to Russia where you belong.'

Terry laughed and replied, 'You've been reading those Tory newspapers again, George. I can always tell by your total lack of constructive argument and the malevolence in your attitude. You've become a proper slave driver in the last few weeks.' Then, as a sudden afterthought, 'The governor hasn't promised you a ship worker's job, has he?'

'Mind your own bloody business, damn you,' George replied.

'Then he has,' said Terry. 'No wonder you've been so belligerent lately – you're turning into a right old governor's man.' He got up and made for the upper 'tween deck hatch, and began climbing down through the 'tween decks into the lower hold, saying, 'Come on, you lot, loosen your chains before George gets his whip out to you.'

*****

Lunchtime came and went; so too did the afternoon and evening tea breaks. By 6.30 that evening the gang had emptied two craft of cement. Then they had to replace the ship's beams and slab hatch covers for the night before they could make their way down the gangway ashore. They were silent now, tired, soaked in perspiration, and covered from head to foot in a grey cement dust that clung to their clothes, to their eyebrows, the ends of their nostrils and their hair. When they stood still they looked to all intents and purposes like stone statues; of course they had to go home in this filthy state, for although Tilbury Docks had been operating for over eighty years, there were no facilities provided for them to wash themselves, or to change their filthy clothes. They would come back to work in the morning dressed in the same clothing as they went home in this evening; most of them would have washed. They were hungry too, and thirsty, very thirsty, as they made their way down the ship's gangway to go wearily home, on foot or on their battered old bicycles.

Some of the men lived locally, while others had to make their way down to Tilbury Riverside Passenger Terminal to catch a ferry boat across the Thames to Gravesend. By the time they had covered up and left the ship it was near to 7 p.m. – and they had to be back aboard the ship by eight o'clock the next morning.

Terry, Brains and several other of the gang, including myself, lived locally, so we made our way to Smoky Joe's café, where we could get ourselves a glass of beer: Joe's unlicensed bar never closed.

Seated as comfortably as we could be on hard wooden benches, and having begun the long task of quenching our parched throats and resting our tired bodies, we began to talk freely. Terry had worked out what we should expect in wages for this day's piecework, plus two overtime hours and an hour's day work, when Brains suddenly asked a question. 'What's a wage slave, Terry?'

Terry smiled. 'The next step up from a serf; and before you ask me what a serf is or was, it was a human chattel somewhere between a slave, a wage earner and a wage slave.'

'Christ, he's off again,' said Charlie. 'Are we going to get a lecture on the dismal subject of wage slavery?'

'If you're not interested in what Terry has got to say about wage slavery, shut your mouth and sod off home,' one of the gang told him. 'We are; so carry on, Terry.'

Terry looked at the faces around the table. Brains looked at Terry expectantly, waiting for him to begin. Terry shrugged his broad shoulders and said, 'Brains asked what a wage slave is, so I'm going to give you my personal interpretation. It's us – the piece-working dockers and stevedores, the colliers, the assembly line workers and any other piece workers who produce the goods and services on which today's modern society relies. I'll begin by giving those of you who may be interested some of the history behind the social changes that have led to the wage slave phenomenon.

'Firstly, it has to be accepted that human beings have always had the propensity not only to enslave animals but also their fellow man. From time immemorial mankind has found ways and means to exploit his fellow man, to benefit at the expense of others.'

'Are you saying we're being exploited, Terry?' interrupted Charlie, lying back on his seat with his eyes half closed. 'We've earned a good day's pay today, we have. There are not many workers who've earned more than us today, I'll bet you.'

'No, you're right there, Charlie,' Terry replied. 'Earned is the operative word, because I bet you no director of P&O, nor any P&O shareholder, is sitting in a dingy bar, drinking pints of lukewarm beer, plastered with cement dust and knackered like we are from the exertion of our labours. No, if they're doing anything they'll be in a comfortable hostelry, sipping pink gin and tonics, or getting dressed up in their finery ready to attend a gala ball at the Freemasons Hall. So close your eyes and go to sleep and let me get on with explaining about wage slavery, right?'

'Yes,' I said, 'shut up or clear off home.' But I was too late. Charlie had closed his eyes and began to snore, out to the world and all that is contained within it.

'Go on, Terry,' said Brains, 'tell us about wage slavery.'

'No, Brains, it would take dozens of books to explain the exploitation of one set of men by another, but I'll give you a rough outline of the various methods used in the past, which have been honed to give us the wage slave methods used by the exploiting employing parasites of today, better known as entrepreneurs; that's a modern name for the wage slave trader.'

'That's your communist bias exerting itself, Terry,' another member of our gang butted in. 'You've got to have, what did you call them, entrepreneurs, or nothing would get done, it stands to reason, don't it?'

'Now to get on with this wage slave philosophy that has been introduced,' said Terry, ignoring the interruption, 'of course it wasn't something that was brought about overnight. It took thousands of years to develop into the art form used today. For example, both the Hittites, an ancient non-Semitic culture of Asia Minor and Syria that appears to have attained a high standard of civilisation before disappearing from history during the seventh century BC, and those peoples who lived in Mesopotamia, the territory between the rivers Euphrates and Tigris that was in pre-classical times the centre of a series of great civilisations that centred on Nineveh, Sumer, Babylon and other great cities of their day, are said to have used various forms of serfdom and slavery to maximise the productive output of human labour.'

'That Nineveh, Terry, is that the same Nineveh mentioned in 'Cargoes' by John Masefield?' Duffy, one of the barge hands, asked.

'Yes, mate, the very same,' replied Terry.

'I love that poem, Terry,' said Brains. '"Quinquireme of Nineveh from distant Ophir, Rowing home to haven in sunny Palestine".'

Terry and the other members of the gang looked at Brains in stunned silence, till Terry said, 'Well done, Brains, I think you may have proved my point with that 'rowing home' phrase in the poem. You see, it was usually slaves that did the rowing – galley slaves.'

'Where would those ancient peoples have got the slaves from, Terry?' I asked.

'I've not the slightest idea,' Terry replied, 'because the Hittite civilisation, as I've already explained to you, disappeared at about the beginning of the seventh century BC. All that is really known about them is that they are mentioned in the Bible, and that many monuments discovered in Asia Minor and in Syria were attributed to that lost civilisation. The Hittites seem to have disappeared after having fought bitter wars for generations with the Egyptians. It could be, though there is no proof of it, that the Egyptians wiped them off the face of the earth.'

Sammy, one of the ship's gang, burst out laughing.

'Have I said something funny?' Terry asked, with a frown on his face.

'Yes! Where did you get that bit about the Bible from, a communist agnostic like you? Everyone knows communists don't read the Bible and don't believe in God.' Sammy was a devout Roman Catholic, except on Sundays when he went to work and missed mass.

'For your information, you bird-brained Bible-punching nincompoop, I use whatever source of information I require in my researches to obtain information. There's a lot of pertinent ancient history in the Bible that can't be obtained anywhere else. Does that answer your question?'

'What's a nincompoop?' said Brains.

'It's a simpleton, an idiot.'

Sammy stood up, glared down at Terry and growled, 'Are you insulting me?'

'In your case I was giving you a compliment. Now sit down and listen or clear off home.' It was a statement supported by menacing mumblings from the rest of us.

'Now,' continued Terry, 'as for the Mesopotamians, it is acknowledged they devised a system of work study and applied time and motion techniques to many work practices. But as to a slave culture being operated, I've not found any concrete proof of that, although I expect it did.'

'Was that a pun, Terry?' Sandy asked with a snigger.

'What do you mean, a pun?'

'You know, a joke. *Concrete* – we've been working on cement all day.'

As the rest of the gang laughed, Terry stroked his chin and stared at the miscreant. Then he said, 'With a name like yours I'd keep my mouth shut when the word cement is mentioned, Sandy. Now give your two operative brain cells a rest while I finish explaining how historians have recorded the origins of the wage slave culture, if that's OK with you.'

'You carry on talking, Terry,' I said. 'I want to know the end of this tale.'

'Thank you for that vote of confidence,' Terry replied. 'In between the Hittite and Mesopotamian periods we know that the Egyptians used vast numbers of slaves in building pyramids and burial chambers for the Pharaohs, because once again it was the Bible that tells us it was Moses who led the Israelites out of slavery in Egypt. So slavery was in vogue long before the Greek and Roman so-called civilisations came into being.'

'Didn't any of the enslaved peoples rise up against those

despots, Terry?' another of the gang asked.

'I suppose there were a number of uprisings over the thousands of years of tyrannical suppression; but the best known and recorded one was that ignited by Spartacus, a Thracian, who was enslaved by the Romans as a gladiator in a place called Capua. He managed to escape from captivity and led a slave insurrection, defeating several Roman armies before he was finally defeated in 71 BC. He was said to have been killed, so the Romans recorded, by a character called Crussus.'

'Yes, a film was made about that. I saw it at the picture house in Grays. A great picture that was,' said Brains. 'But what's the difference between a slave and a serf?'

'How is it that it's you, Brains, that asks me the more sensible questions? After all, you're the one none of these others thinks is too bright,' said Terry.

Brains smiled, shrugged his shoulders, then said, 'I was studying accountancy before the war, but after I was blown up on Sword Beach during the Normandy landings I've not been able to focus my mind properly, but I'm still interested in things, all things.'

Terry was far too dumbfounded to reply. He and Brains had become firm friends over the last few years, but neither had questioned the other about his past history; that was something one never did in the docks, and we never found out much about our workmates unless they cared for reasons of their own to volunteer such information, as Brains had just done. The rest of us sat in silence, utterly surprised by Brains' submission, and not wishing to show how we had underrated the former mental capability of this workmate. Some of us had spent a goodly part of our time using him as a scapegoat for our own inadequacies, denigrating him for his slow wittedness and using him as the butt for our jokes. That would never happen again. Brains would from then on be seen in a different light. He was one of our fraternity – truly one of us.

Terry broke the ice. 'Well, Brains, as to your question about the difference between a slave and a serf, the answer is there wasn't a great deal of difference. It was more or less that a serf was born into serfdom. He couldn't be bought or sold like a slave, but he couldn't marry without his lord's permission. He was required to till his lord's fields, gather his crops and fight for him if necessary; a serf's wife and daughters also had to do unpaid work, being obliged to work in the fields and help with the indoor work at the manor house, including wool spinning, weaving, sewing, baking and brewing. Those people were born to serfs, lived the life of a serf, and they died as serfs.'

'But why didn't the serfs rebel?' Sandy asked.

'For the same reason that we don't rebel. You see, people born into any form of social system accept that system as being the norm, until something untoward happens. Under a feudal system nothing changed, because their situation was inherited within a rigid class structure. The serf was born into a feudal system; you on the other hand were born into a wage-slave social system. You may not like to think it, but you were. Slaves, on the other hand, were either born into slavery through their parents having been slaves, or they were captured and taken by force into slavery. Many of the slaves were of high social standing in their own tribes or communities, and quite possibly had owned slaves themselves. Those were the ones that took umbrage at becoming slaves. These were the ones who were most likely to rebel against being held as slaves, but with the exception of Spartacus, I don't know of any slaves who rebelled.'

'Do you know what caused the feudal system to break down, Terry?' Sandy asked.

'No! No one can say for sure, but my guess would be two major events. First was the Jacquerie: that was an uprising by French peasants in 1358; and second was the outbreak of bubonic plague in Europe in 1348.'

'Why was that?'

'Because, although there may have been other uprisings in France before 1358 which were not recorded, this one was followed in England, after the bubonic plague had wiped out a large percentage of the English population, by the English peasants' revolt led by Wat Tyler in 1381.'

'But what about the wage slave theory, Terry?' said Albert. 'How did that come about?'

'Well, up to the time of the Black Death the majority of

those workers who cultivated the land belonged to a particular manor. They paid dues to their manor's lord by performing duties for him. There were very few hired farmhands seeking employment in that period of history. The plague, however, by decimating the number of labourers available for hire, raised wages and thereby served to increase the importance attached to labouring jobs generally. The consequence of this was that labourers not only demanded higher wages, but they readily left one employer for another when offered more money.'

'Do you lot know what time it is?' Rosie, one of Smokey Joe's 'girls' who was acting as barmaid, called out to us. 'It's eleven o'clock and all of you look as though you could do with a good bath and a decent meal.'

'Holy Mary,' Sandy said, 'I'm in trouble when I get home. If I know her indoors, my dinner will be in the yob.'

Terry laughed. 'You mean in that fat lazy son of yours?'

'You've got it in one, mate,' Sandy replied as he scuttled out of the café's back door and disappeared into the gloomy cold night air.

We all got up to go except Sid, who was still fast asleep.

'Give that lazy sod a kick and wake him up,' said Terry, so Brains did just that as the rest of us filed out of Smokey Joe's to the sound of 'You shower of bastards,' to which someone laughingly replied, 'How does he know that? Has he been doing a bit of genealogy on us?'

*****

On the following morning at eight o'clock a weary gang of dockers, some now suffering from lack of sleep as well as from the previous day's physical exertions, congregated on the ship's deck and began stripping off the ship's hatches, ready for me, high above them in my crane cabin, to lower the crane hook down to them so they could shackle the wire beam spreaders to remove the ship's beams in order to gain access to the lower hold, ready to commence loading the next consignment of cement. However, I could not help noticing from my perch up in the sky that although the men were washed and clean, they were wearing the same togs as they had been the day before, covered with cement dust.

There was nothing unusual about this, for although washing machines had been invented, ordinary working men employed in filthy occupations, such as the docks, refuse collection and coal mining, could not afford such luxuries for their wives. So cement dust would stay on their clothes till the cement job was finished and they began to load general cargo. Then their wives would gather up the heavily cement-impregnated clobber, after it had been bashed against a brick wall to knock out the worst of the cement dust, and take it to a local laundrette where it would be cleaned. After this it would be taken home and patched or re-patched. Some of the men used their old and endlessly repaired service battle-dresses as working clothes; clothing that reminded one of the patched rags worn by displaced persons, refugees and former concentration camp prisoners who had wandered aimlessly about Europe at the end of the Second World War. Constant repair made these rags ready for their next encounter with the filth and grime of cargoes from many countries round the world.

By the time the ship's down-holders had stripped the hatch covers off the beams, removed the beams and sister beams from the hatch combing, clambered down through the 'tween deck hatchways into the lower hold, it was 8.20 a.m., and I had a set of cement hanging over their heads ready for them to begin working. I soon got into a regular work pattern, working end-on-end out of a Thames lighter with thirty-two bags of cement in each load, and lowering it into the ship's port and starboard wings alternately.

This routine was carried on till 9.30 a.m., when Brains called out the traditional breaktime call of 'Beer Ho'. Then the down-holders climbed wearily back up from the lower hold into the upper 'tween deck. I climbed from the crane cabin, clambered down the vertical steel ladders onto the quay and made my way up the ship's gangway, while at the same time the barge hands climbed out of the Thames lighter and followed me up the gangway onto the ship's deck.

There was never usually very much said by the men during their tea breaks; they were too busy eating their sandwiches and drinking their tea. But on this occasion

Terry's previous evening lecture on wage slavery was being discussed by all those who had been at Smokey Joe's Café.

When I arrived, I was just in time to hear George say, 'He's a bloody communist anarchist, that's what he is. Always on about a fair day's pay for a fair day's work.'

'By Christ, George,' said Sandy, 'you've changed your tune, haven't you? Not long ago you would have been agreeing with Terry on that one.'

Terry, sitting on his own on the stringer boards as usual, laughed. Then he said, 'He would be now, but the Old Man's offered him a ship worker's job, hasn't he, George?'

George stood up and looked down menacingly at Terry. 'So what? Someone's got to do it.'

'I know,' said Terry, 'that's what the prostitute told the bishop.'

It was at this point that Charlie called down the hold, 'George, it's started to rain. Get the lads up on deck and rig the dolly-brook. Henry, get back up in the crane and put the lighter-man's barge beams on for him.'

'Damn the weather,' I heard George say as I climbed up through the deck hatchway. 'I was hoping to get the port and starboard wings filled in this morning, so we could have an easy afternoon filling in the square of the hatch.'

For those of you who don't know, a dolly-brook is a large tent used on cargo boats, which covers a ship's hatch to prevent rain getting on the cargo. It's held in place by hooking the top of the canopy onto the end of a winch wire, then hoisting the top up to the derrick's head by means of a ship's winch; the rope tails are then lashed onto the outer rim of the hatch combing to make it secure. When the dolly-brook is fully rigged, it's as if a large marquee has been erected on the ship's deck.

It did not take us long to get the ship closed up. Then we made our way back down through the deck hatch into the upper 'tween deck, where four of the other gang members had already rigged up a couple of light clusters, made themselves a table out of the wooden deck hatch covers and were playing a hand of bridge – a game I was never intelligent enough to get the hang of. But I sat watching them for a short time, listening to them as they spoke of 'tricks', 'dummies' and 'grand slams'.

Then I heard Sandy's voice call across the open hatch to Terry. 'Will you carry on telling us about your wage slave theory, Terry?'

Terry got up from his isolated perch. We could see his outline in the half light from the electric cluster lamps that were being used by the card school, and walked across to where the rest of the gang were congregated. 'Right,' he said, 'how far did I get last night?'

'Where bubonic plague had wiped out most of the serfs who had been tied to the lords of the manor, and how serfdom began to disappear as labourers began to demand money payments for their services,' Brains said.

'Ah yes,' said Terry. 'So how did the ruling classes react to this dilemma?'

'Well, how did they react?' said Sandy.

'They simply passed an Act of Parliament to suppress wage demands. The Act was called the Statute of Labourers, and its objective was to prohibit labourers from asking for higher wages than the aristocrats and landed gentry had been accustomed to pay during the years that had preceded the plague, on pain of imprisonment. The first Statute of Labourers was passed in 1351, but it was not fully complied with, and similar laws were enacted from time to time for a hundred years.'

Charlie butted in with, 'Never mind about that. What happened next?'

'I've already told you, cloth ears. The old manorial system was breaking up. The villeins, as the serfs were called in England, began to regard the dues they had been accustomed to pay their lords as unjust. The lords had the opposite attitude, unsurprisingly, and sent a petition to Parliament in 1377, asserting that their villeins were refusing to pay their customary dues and services, or acknowledge the obligations they owed as serfs.'

'The revolting, lazy blackguards,' Sandy said.

Charlie laughed and replied, 'Just like you, Sandy, when you go on strike.'

'That's different. When I go on strike it's for a good reason.'

'Sandy,' interjected Terry, 'it's for the same reason, but

under different circumstances.'

Charlie butted in with, 'Get on with it, Terry. What happened next?'

'Exactly,' replied Terry. '*Wat* happened next; it was *Wat Tyler*. First there was a revolt by the Men of Kent and Kentish Men in 1381, led by Wat Tyler. That was against taxes being levied on the peasants to carry on a war with France. Don't forget, Kent had its own laws that were negotiated at the time of the Norman Conquest, and the Kentish people possibly felt they had a right to object at what they saw as an unjust tax imposed on them, although I've never seen this mentioned in any history book. However, a subsequent rebellion by Kentish people under Jack Cade, an Irish adventurer who led an insurrection in Kent against Henry VI in 1450, was simply to demand that the king should redress the people's grievances. Both those uprisings were put down by force, and most of the perpetrators and leaders were either struck down, as was the case with Wat Tyler, or strung up when they were arrested.

'However, the seeds for social and economic change within England and France had been sown. In France it was with devastating consequences for King Louis XVI and the French aristocrats, who lost their heads to the guillotine after the French Revolution. There was to be no turning back. Serfdom and slavery would succumb to the reality of social and economic progress, but this in turn would herald a new labour control, time and motion study work practices, the wage slave era coupled with mass production, the piece workers – and us; but I'll come to the bogeyman of controlled work practices later.'

'But did it, Terry? Did it change the system?' Brains asked.

'No it didn't, at least not immediately,' Terry replied, 'but it did change the wage payment system for what was to become known as the working class, changing them from slaves and serfs to wage earners.'

'What do you determine to be a wage earner, Terry?' George butted in. 'Are you referring to all working people?'

'No. There are several different forms of wage payment. For example, the clergy are paid a stipend; that's a fixed periodic money payment for work done within the Church. Then there's the fee, a sum paid to lawyers, doctors and some other self-employed professionals, and no, it won't be you, George, when you get promoted to ship worker: you'll be what is known as a member of the salaried staff category of employees, with an income paid to you monthly and a pension when you retire. In other words you'll be other than a manual worker, like what we are.'

'You bloody turncoat, George,' Sandy said.

George shrugged his shoulders and smiled, then he said, 'Watch your tongue, Sandy. I'll be picking gangs up in the Dock Labour Compound next week, when our ship worker Charlie is on his holidays. I may not see you when you shape up on "the call".'

All went quiet with that threat. You could hear the ship's rats scampering and squeaking as they fought each other for the scraps of bread thrown down in the scuppers. Suddenly there was a loud clap of thunder that rolled around the heavens above the ship, coupled with the sound of heavy rain slapping against the sail cloth of the dolly-brook directly over our heads, and the infernal dripping as raindrops cascaded off the dolly-brook, forcing droplets of water under the outer cover of the sail cloth to run down the inside of the hatch combing and drip onto the upper 'tween deck ceiling.

The silence was broken when George said, 'Brains, go up on deck and secure the lashing where the rain's coming in.'

'Stay where you are, Brains,' Terry said. 'We aren't serfs now, nor are we slaves, nor will we be blackmailed by your threats. You go and tie the lashing up yourself, George. Forget you were a sergeant major, long ago, when you were in the army.'

George's face went the colour of the midday sun on the equator, but he stood up, smiled and walked across the 'tween deck, climbing up through the hatch cover opening, out into the pouring rain, to tie the loose rope's end himself. He knew he had lost face with the gang, because of his threat to Sandy. They were men he had worked with for several years, men who had respected him as their leader, but now they had doubts about his loyalty to them.

Sandy said, 'Bloody fine thing when a workmate

threatens you like that. What do you think, Terry?'

Terry shrugged his shoulders and said, 'Take it with a pinch of salt, Sandy. George was only bluffing. It was his way of showing us who he thinks is going to be boss when he becomes a ship worker.'

It was at this point that George called down the open deck hatch, 'Go to lunch and be back aboard here at 1 p.m. sharp. The clouds are breaking up and it looks as if we'll be able to restart work. See you then.'

And before any of us had time to crawl up through the hatch opening onto the deck George had vanished ashore. His battered old pre-war bicycle had gone; there was not a sign of him anywhere.

Terry said, 'The bloody fool, that promise of a ship worker's job has gone to his head already. Let's see what he does when he comes back to work this afternoon.'

They left it at that – for the time being at least.

2

Rosie Taunts Terry

When we members of the ship's gang arrived back on board it was 1.05 p.m. The weather had improved; the rain had stopped although it was still overcast with heavy cloud cover. The lighterman had already removed the tarpaulins and hatch covers from his craft's stowage bays, and had piled them on the fore and aft sections of his lighter. George was already aboard, busy untying the rope ends that held the dolly-brook in place around the ship's hatch combing. We, as a ship's gang, were well behind our own target of tonnage. We had set ourselves the task of loading a minimum of 300 tons of cement a day, but we had only managed to load eighty tons before the rain had set in. So, in order to catch up, we decided the barge hands would put thirty-six bags of cement in each loading net, instead of the usual thirty-two. By this means we hoped to raise the tonnage figure to a more acceptable level of piecework production. It was a discussion from which George stood aloof, and to which he made no contribution.

Now I have to be honest and state I was against the idea, the reason being it was bad psychological practice. It created greater fatigue among the barge hands, as they had an empty cement net hanging over their heads and began to struggle to catch up. For them it was demoralising, which eventually

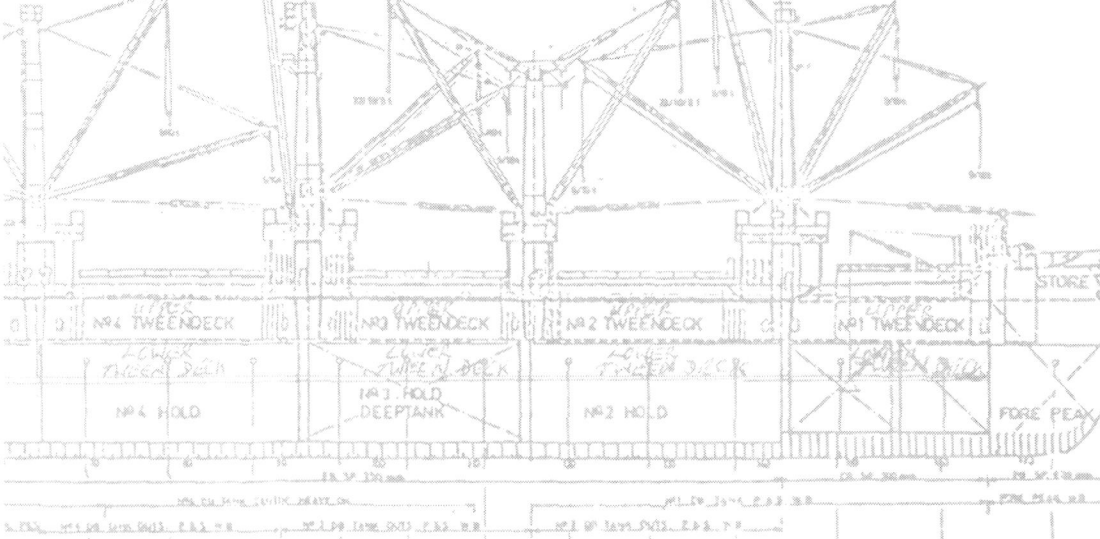

began to slow them down. However, they (the workers) were doing all the physical labour, so I was over-ruled, of course.

At this stage George hadn't spoken to any member of the gang, nor had they spoken to him, until Terry taunted him. 'Are you going to sulk for the rest of the day, George, or are you going to take charge and decide what we are going to do next? A bloody fine ship worker you'll turn out to be.'

George had, of course, been listening to every word of our conversation, but Terry's remarks motivated him into action. He suddenly barked out in his sergeant major's voice, 'Someone get on that winch and lower the dolly brook down into the upper 'tween deck. Henry, you get up in the crane and take the beams off the lighter. Albert and Duffy, you two go into the lighter with the barge hands. We're working in the square of the hold and we can manage with four down-holders till the hatch square is filled. We'll give it a go till "Beer Ho". There's eighty tons in that lighter; that's 1,600 bags of cement. If we do thirty-six to each set we load that's forty-five sets. One set every two minutes means we can finish that craft by half past two, if we take a late tea break. Is that what you wanted to hear, Terry?'

'That's it,' Terry replied.

'Right then, you all know what to do, so damn well get on with it. By the way, Henry, before you luff the crane's jib out to take the lighter's beams off, pick the cement nets up off the quay and take them over to the lighter. It'll give the barge hands time to make up the first sets of cement.'

It is interesting, from a psychological point of view, to note just how important camaraderie is within social groups, how one misfit can jeopardise the cohesiveness of a whole unit. George, having been brought to his senses by Terry, got on with doing what he was best at, being in charge, and he set the gang back on track to achieve their target, which they failed to do that day by only twenty tons.

I did exactly as I was bid and within minutes, as the barge hands banged bags of cement down onto the cement nets, a halo of grey cement dust floated up over the lighter, like a thick early morning smog. As I watched and waited (perched as I was in my crane cabin high up in the sky) for the signal to lower the crane hook to lift the first set of cement out of the craft. I thought, what a bloody horrible way for human beings to have to earn a livelihood.

This performance went on till 6.30 that evening, after we had emptied two more lighters, and forty tons out of a Thames sailing barge. But the barge skipper called a halt to the proceedings when he realised we wouldn't complete the discharge of his craft before we knocked off work. Had we been able to do so, he would have been able to float his barge over to the lock gates and out into the river, ready to catch the falling tide to return to Cliffe cement works jetty, to pick up another barge load of cement.

Barge skippers were paid freightage, which was calculated by the number of freight loads they delivered to ships or merchants. It was another form of piecework for which they often took unwarranted risks with their craft, and their lives.

We had to cover up the ship's hatch anyway, put the beams, hatch covers and tarpaulins on and make them secure before the gang left the ship.

It was almost 7 p. m. as I put the crane fore and aft to the quay and climbed out of the cabin and down the vertical steel ladders, and the last of the men walked slowly down the ship's gangway, ready for a drink and a rest.

As Terry and the rest of us walked into Smokey Joe's back room, his illegal bar, Rosie was once again the serving wench. She was wearing a low cut dress (I do mean low, almost down to her navel), and was leaning over the bar counter exposing her ample bosom. She smiled at Terry, winked and asked, 'What can I do for you, Terry darling?'

'Just a pint of Uncle Joe's ice-cold, lukewarm beer of dubious origin and manufacture, please, Rosie.'

Rosie wriggled her breasts on the bar counter, looked Terry straight in the eye and asked, 'Are you gay, Terry, or what?'

'That's a queer thing to say to a docker who's just been castrated by loading hundreds of bags of cement in a ship's hold, who's thirsty, hungry, tired and, to be truthful, shagged-out.'

'That's the trouble with you young dockers these days, no stamina. If that's what working on cement does for you, I think I'll carry on working for Joe.'

'Yes, it's no contest, Rosie,' said Terry, 'being humped is by far better than humping. What's more it's probably far more pleasurable, and it pays better too.'

'Not when you work for Joe it isn't. Some of us girls have to do a bit of moonlighting to make ends meet,' Rosie said, as she passed Terry his beer; then, without saying another word, she served the rest of us, and we made our way slowly and silently to the far corner of the bar and slumped down on the hard wooden benches. 'What do you expect, when you come in here in that state – wall-to-wall carpets and easy chairs?' Smokey Joe would say, waving his arms about, if anybody complained about the seating arrangements. 'Isn't the beer cheap enough as it is?' Then, as if close to tears, he would say, 'On my life, lads, I do my best for you, don't I do my best for you?' And he'd walk out from behind the bar into his back room mumbling to himself. . . .

Slowly we began to gulp down our pints, as Rosie looked on from behind the bar with a sympathetic expression on her pretty round face. She was no doubt thinking of her husband, who had been severely injured in a dock accident and was no longer able to work. With two children to support, she was forced to do the only job her education fitted her for, working in Smokey Joe's illicit back room emporium and acting as a white geisha girl to all and sundry.

After we had sat in silence for a short time emptying our glasses, and one by one had made our way back to the bar for a re-charge, Brains said, 'Are you going to tell us a bit more about wage slavery, Terry?'

'Yes, if you're sure you want me to. Now how far did I get before we were rudely interrupted by George in the 'tween deck?'

'George asked what you determined to be wage slavery,' Sandy reminded him.

'Ah, yes! But I've already explained the difference between a slave and a serf. Perhaps it would be useful if I tell you how serfdom was introduced into England. It came about after the Norman invasion in 1066. For although there were known to be military tenures in England during Saxon times, it's certain that such tenures underwent many alterations after the Norman Conquest, with the extension of numerous feudal customs being introduced to suppress and supervise the indigenous population. These changes in the social structure were introduced specifically for the benefit of the newly created classes of aristocracy put in place by William the Conqueror to strengthen his control over the country. But as I explained to you last evening, that system began to collapse after the outbreak of bubonic plague.'

'So are you saying, Terry, that serfdom and slavery came to an end after the bubonic plague?' I asked.

'No I'm not, Henry. Serfdom went into decline only after the serfs began to pay their dues to the lords in money, instead of working for him. It was in this way that the serfs began to lose the characteristics of being serfs, and the lords became landlords – renting out their lands to former serfs who became tenant yeoman farmers. It was in this way that sixty or seventy years after the Peasants' Revolt the English rural population had in one way or another become free men. Serfdom had to all intents and purposes disappeared.'

'But what about slavery, Terry, had that disappeared?' Brains asked.

'No, not at that time it hadn't. From an historical point of view, the Portuguese had began slave trading from Ghana in the seventeenth century, then during the eighteenth and nineteenth centuries Britain set up trading settlements. Assisted by the Ashanti tribal rulers who controlled the land between the Volta river and the Togo mountains, they actively participated in a slave trade that shipped thousands of Africans to the Caribbean islands to work in the sugar cane fields, and to the Southern American states to work in the cotton plantations. To all intents and purposes in England slavery had been abolished, with a few minor exceptions, but there were still slave compounds in the ports of Bristol and Liverpool, where slaves were brought from Africa to be sold to American and Caribbean sugar and cotton plantation owners.'

'Terry,' Sandy said, 'you mentioned slavery had disappeared in England, but with a few minor exceptions. What were the exceptions?'

'Can't you guess? My lady of the manor liked to have a little black boy or girl dressed up to the nines in fine clothes, with a jewelled silver or gold collar round the neck as a token of dependence, a child that would follow her around like a pet poodle. The Duchess of Queensberry had a black boy whom she called Soubise, who was educated and instructed in the accomplishments of a gentleman. King William III had a slave who wore a padlocked white marble collar round his neck, and even criminals were known to have had slaves. There is on record John Rice, convicted as a forger, who was hanged at Tyburn in 1767. When his personal effects were auctioned, among them was his Negro boy who was sold for £32. In 1769 Granville Sharp published a pamphlet on slavery called *The Injustice and Dangerous Tendency of Tolerating Slavery in England*, after he had saved a slave boy, Jonathan Strong, who had been beaten and half blinded by his master, a David Lisle of Barbados.

'Granville Sharp, who has never been given the full credit he deserves in the abolition of slavery, came up with a watertight case against it in 1772. The case revolved round a Negro by the name of Somerset, whose master had him clapped in irons and put on board a ship in the Thames. Sharp intervened and Somerset was brought before the King's Bench, where Lord Chief Justice Mansfield tried the case. He did his best to wriggle out of giving a humane decision, but he finally delivered this historic judgement: "The state of slavery is so odious that nothing can be suffered to support it but positive law. Whatever inconvenience, therefore, may fall from this decision, I cannot say this case is allowed or approved by the law of England."'

'Are you telling us there was no law passed to set the serfs free in England, but a law had to be passed to outlaw slavery?' asked Charlie. Then as an afterthought he asked, 'How many freed slaves were there, and what happened to them when they were freed?'

'The number was estimated at about fourteen thousand, and Granville Sharp, their benefactor, was quickly beleaguered by many of those he had been responsible for setting free.'

'What did he do about it?' interrupted Sandy.

'He was offered a ship that would take them overseas to found a new colony of free black men. He accepted the proposal, and in 1787 a ship left the river Thames with the first consignment of over four hundred ex-slaves and sixty white women from Wapping, who had been made drunk and kidnapped for the occasion. The ship made for the west coast of Africa to form the colony of Sierra Leone.'

'Are you telling us that this Granville Sharp went through all that trouble to free the slaves held in England, then entrapped white women against their will to accompany the ex-slaves to Sierra Leone?' I asked.

'Yes, he did.'

'No wonder then that William Wilberforce grabbed most of the anti-slavery kudos. What a bloody despicable thing to do to women of your own race,' said Sandy.

'Bloody typical, I call it,' said Charlie.

'Did that put an end to slavery in England?' Brains asked.

'In England, quite possibly yes. But it certainly extended the wage-earning fraternity to cover all manual labour, and that must have included the ex-slaves.'

'You lot will get ex-slaves when you get home,' Rosie called from behind the bar. 'It's after eleven o'clock and your wives will think you're all dead, or something.'

'They'll think it's "or something" if we tell them we've been in Smokey Joe's back room with you,' said Terry.

'Go on, go home you lot,' Rosie ordered them. 'You're beginning to look like gargoyles on a Gothic cathedral.' And like children who'd been chastised by their schoolteacher, we got up and filed silently out of Smokey Joe's café, into the cold night air.

*****

The following morning, at eight o'clock, a scruffy and dishevelled group of dockers, dressed in their cement dust-caked working togs, huddled together inside the transit shed adjacent to the loading ship. They were grumbling because the ship's gangway had been removed. The fore and aft springs that held her to the quay bollards had been slackened off, and a dummy pontoon was being laboriously dragged by two Port Authority tugboat crew men, between the ship and the quay to a point at mid-ships.

The simple reason for this manoeuvre by the shipping company was so that lighters and sailing barges could be brought between the ship and quay, therefore allowing double banking gangs to work over-side under derricks, while at the same time gangs using quay cranes could operate from craft between the ship and the quay. Nobody could get aboard the ship till the dummy was secured and the ship's gangway had been put back in place.

All of those who had been drinking in Smokey Joe's café the previous evening, and had been listening to Terry's 'slaves and wage slaves lecture', had gone home to a severe lashing from the tongues of their wives – who had had to keep their meals heated, but had also lived in the dreaded anticipation of a knock on the door by a police constable to tell them, 'He won't be home tonight, had a bit of an accident, he's in hospital,' or worse.

Now they were back at work, safe from their worried nagging wives, they could be themselves among battle-hardened, work-toughened contemporaries, who had all suffered the same fate.

'Sod you, Terry,' said Sandy, 'I got a real earful from my old woman when I got home last night.'

'Yes, so did I,' said Charlie. 'What about you, Brains?'

'No, not I,' replied Brains. 'Sophie just said, "you're rather late tonight, Jonathan. Have you had a hard day again today?" Then she waited for me to clean myself up, put my dinner on the table and . . .'

'OK. We don't want to hear about it chapter and verse. So you didn't get, what's the word I'm looking for, Terry?' Sandy asked.

'Castigated,' Terry replied.

'Bollocked is the word I was trying to think of,' said Sandy.

'What's the difference between those two words?' Brains asked.

'Castigated simply means to be told off or reprimanded; castrated means for a male animal to have its testicles removed, cut off,' Terry explained.

'No! Sophie wouldn't do that to me,' said Brains. It was a comment that brought a bout of laughter from the rest of us.

*****

Unfortunately, placing the dummy between the quay and the ship took longer than expected. This was because another ship was leaving the docks through the lock gates, and the wash from its propellers jammed our ship fast against the dummy, and the dummy fast against the quay wall. It wasn't till the backwash coming off our ship allowed her to drift away from the dummy that the tugboat men, now assisted by frustrated dockers trying to get aboard our ship, were able to get the dummy mid-ships and secured her to quayside bollards, and the ship's lascar deck crew could lower the vessel's own gangway onto the dummy's decking. It was now 8.45 a.m., and my gang members were soon hurrying up the ship's gangway to take off the hatch covers, making ready for me to remove the steel beams and sister beams.

When I had climbed up the vertical steel ladders and was at the controls of the crane, I noticed the sailing barge skipper and his mate had uncovered their barge's hatches and had loaded five of the cement nets themselves. It was then I remembered they were trying to catch the ebb tide to take them down river, so as soon as the gang had finished clearing the hatchway and I had removed the ship's deck hatch beams I slewed the crane's jib over the barge, lifted the barge beam out of its central coupling, placed it on the barge combing, picked up the first set of cement from the barge and had it down the ship's lower hold within a couple of minutes.

As the first set of cement came to rest on the landing bed, George turned to Terry and said, 'Sixty tons, Terry, that's twelve hundred bags, or about thirty-eight sets, isn't it? What do you think, should we empty the barge before we go to "Beer Ho"?'

'Absolutely, George,' Terry replied, 'then the lighter-man can change the craft over while we have our tea break. That will help cut out the time we've lost and bump up our tonnage rate.'

Those were the last words spoken till Old Joe, the top-hand, shouted down the hatchway, 'Four sets left in the barge.'

George told Brains, 'Go up and make the tea. We should be up in the 'tween deck in about ten minutes.' The time was 9.45 a.m.

Old Joe rarely came down the hold to get a cup of tea. He was in his late sixties or early seventies, and suffered terribly from arthritis in his knees that caused him to walk like a clockwork toy. Some of the gang joked that his disability was due to his begging Charlie, the ship worker, for his cushy job, but it was in fact due to a serious shipboard accident some years before, when both his legs had been crushed by a set of timber. So Brains poured Joe's tea into a glass lemonade bottle (with three spoonfuls of sugar added), which Joe pulled up onto the deck by means of a length of string, which was coiled up and stowed in the gang's tea-box when it was not in use. There was also a bottle attached to a piece of string for me. Brains would pour my tea into the lemonade bottle, the string was placed over the crane's hook and I would hoist the bottle up and swing it into the cabin through the open window – a clever but precarious trick, considering the ball of the crane itself weighed some five hundredweight.

It was about twenty minutes after the gang had stopped work for their tea break when Old Joe called down the hatch, 'Lighter's under plumb, George, 120 tons. Charlie told me to tell you to get that loaded by tonight, because that'll complete the cement for the lower hold. He's ordered up the wood dunnage to overstow the cement, ready for the casework, vehicles and heavy lifts.'

'Right, Joe,' George called back to him; then he asked Terry, 'How many sets?'

'Seventy-one,' Terry replied.

'How long to empty the lighter?' George asked.

'About 140 minutes. It's five past ten now, a quarter past ten before we can get started, say a hour and a half this morning, which should see at least sixty tons stowed aboard. That'll leave sixty tons for after lunch,' Terry replied.

'What time should we clear that lighter by?'

'About half past two.'

'Right, let's get to it then,' and one by one the gang made their separate way down the ship's vertical steel ladder into the lower hold. The barge hands followed me up through the deck hatchway, they on their way to the lighter filled with cement, and me up into the crane cabin to lift the cement nets into the lighter and to remove the lighter's beam. Suffice it for me to state, we finished discharging the lighter at 2.30, Brains made the tea and we sat waiting for two hours for the lorries fetching the sawn wood dunnage to turn up, during which time Terry was asked to continue his lecture about wage slavery.

'Well', Terry began, 'I think I got up to about 1772, when Lord Chief Justice Mansfield was forced to acknowledge that slavery was odious, and made his momentous judgement that ended slavery in England. It was that decision that really brought about the wage payments system.'

'So was that the end of slavery, Terry?' Brains asked.

'In England, yes,' Terry agreed, 'but slavery as such was still a worldwide scourge. Mansfield's judgement only affected those slaves who were held in England. It had no power abroad, although it was to eventually have worldwide implications.'

'In what way?' asked Sandy.

'Through the efforts of other men, who were equally appalled by the bloody minded temerity of the slave trading industry,' Terry replied.

'Who, for example?' said Sandy

'Well,' said Terry, 'the names of James Ramsay and John Newton first spring to mind.'

'Who were they?' said Charlie.

'James Ramsay was a man of Scottish extraction, who trained as a doctor's assistant in London. He joined the navy in 1757, no doubt to work on improving his surgical skills, practising on matelots who became casualties in battles with Caribbean pirates.'

'I love that poem about pirates,' interjected Brains.

'What poem is that?' Terry asked in the gentle voice he used when speaking to Brains.

'The Last Buccaneer,' Brains replied.

Who wrote it, and how does it go?' said Terry.

'It was written by Charles Kingsley, a clergyman,' said Brains; then to everyone's surprise he began, '"Oh, England is a pleasant place for them that's rich and high, But England is a cruel place for such poor folk as I, And such a place for mariners I ne'er shall see again, As the pleasant Isle of Aves, beside the Spanish Main."'

'Yes,' said Duffy, one of the barge hands, 'and to support your argument on slavery it goes on, "Oh, the palms grew high in Aves, and the fruits that shone like gold, And the coleus and the parrots they were gorgeous to behold, And the Negro maids to Aves from bondage fast did flee, To welcome gallant sailors, a-sweeping in from the sea."'

'Does either of you know how the poem ends?' asked Terry; and to everyone's surprise Albert, Duffy's mate in the barge who all and sundry took to be a dunderhead, butted in with, '"And now I'm old and going – I'm sure I can't tell where, One comfort is, this world's so hard, I can't be worse off there, If I might be a sea dove, I'd fly across the main, To the pleasant Isle of Aves, to look at it once again."'

'Well, I never did!' Terry exclaimed in utter surprise. 'I'm astounded. All the years I've known you lot, and I had no inkling that any of you had so much as a glimmer of a soul! Where did you learn that part of the poem, Albert?'

'From my granddad, just before he was taken to a workhouse before the war,' Albert replied.

'Get on with your story, Terry,' Old Joe said. 'I never get to hearing anything like this when I'm up on deck.'

'OK, Joe,' said Terry. 'Now how far did I get?'

'James Ramsay joined the navy to get some surgical experience practising on sailors injured in battles with pirates,' Albert said.

'Oh yes! However, following an injury to himself, James Ramsay left the navy and took holy orders in the Church of England. He was given a parish on the island of St Kitts in the Caribbean. It was on St Kitts that he witnessed at first hand the cruel treatment meted out to slaves by slave masters employed by the Church of England. Ramsay's open objection to the cruelty resulted in him being boycotted by the white slave masters, and he was forced to return to England to seek a living.'

'What happened to him?' Charlie asked.

'He became the vicar of a village in Kent. From there he continued his anti-slavery campaign, and wrote essays about the cruel treatment of African slaves in the British sugar-producing colonies.'

'What about the other bloke, John Newton?' said Old Joe.

'Actually he was the Reverend John Newton, Rector of St Mary Woolworth. As a young man he had been press ganged as a midshipman in the navy, and had been involved in the African slave trade. His experiences led him into taking holy orders; then in 1779 he met and became a friend of William Wilberforce and William Cowper, a poet. It was in the main through their efforts and those of many other virtuous but anonymous campaigners that John Newton became involved in the anti-slavery campaign.'

'So it wasn't Wilberforce who started the anti-slavery movement, as we have always been led to believe?' said Sandy.

'No! Not by a long shot,' exclaimed Terry. 'Wilberforce was a member of parliament who voiced to the House of Commons the anti-slavery movement's misgivings about the use of slaves as a means of labour production. You see, slavery's virtual abolition in England in 1772 was followed by Denmark's decision to prohibit slave trading within its territories in 1792. It was then only a matter of time before other nations relented and abolished the trade, and so it was with great reluctance that parliament abolished slavery in most countries of the British Empire in 1807. I say most countries of the British Empire because India, for example, didn't abolish slavery till 1838. This was quite possibly because politicians were brought to realise the long-term benefits that would accrue from its abolition.'

'So slavery was finally abolished, was it?' Old Joe asked.

'Of course not,' said Terry, 'it just changed its form. There will never be an end to slavery as there will never be an end to serfdom. Those two evils have taken on a different mantle in these so-called enlightened days, and shall pursue their victims till eternity or the demise of mankind itself.'

'And what have those forms taken?' I asked.

'What is termed a free labour market, as you should all well know from your personal experiences of the Dock Labour Board's system of surplus of manpower and the "free for all" or "every man for himself" when jobs turn up in the Dock Labour Compound.'

'How do employers get such a system to operate?' said Cyril.

'By a number of different methods,' replied Terry, 'but specifically through basic need, through the fear of being without basic needs, and social persecution – seeing what the Joneses have got and you have not.'

'How do the exploiters do this?' asked Sandy.

'Simply by keeping wealth-producing workers' wages low, and continually encouraging an influx of cheap labour into working areas of production, to continuously create a surplus of labour. These are the tools of repression used by the exploiters of labour; the entrepreneurial cast that is forever on a quest for cheap labour to suppress wages and create fear of unemployment, which forces the workers to produce more and therefore greater profits. The entrepreneurs' main tool in today's labour market is employment agencies; that is, agencies that hire out workers, in many cases to major employers, or in our case shipping companies and dock labour contractors through the Dock Labour Boards. This is all done in order to minimise wages and maximise profits, without employers having to contribute to pension funds or other future benefits that employees should expect to receive under current legislation when they retire from paid employment.'

'But hasn't anyone tried to do anything about it?' Old Joe asked.

'Well oddly enough, in the past the answer to that question is yes, and from the most unlikely sources. These include a factory manager by the name of Robert Owen. Owen became the manager, then the owner, of a cotton mill at New Lanark, a factory he managed on good old socialist and profit-sharing principles. He began a system of education before the advent of the workhouse apprentice for children of the workers he employed; he also improved the housing and sanitary conditions of the hovels in which his workers lived. His socialist creed was embodied in essays such as his 'New View of Society, The New Moral World'. He tried a similar exercise in America in 1825, but that was a failure because it attracted many non-producing intellectual layabouts. Owen also pioneered infant education, as well as helping to set up co-operative societies.

Another name that springs to mind is that of Lord Shaftesbury. Shaftesbury was a philanthropist, as well as being a Conservative politician. He supported the Ragged School movement, began by John Pound of Portsmouth in 1820, a movement that gave free education and succour to destitute children. Pound, with Lord Shaftesbury's support, developed the Ragged School Union in 1844, and the Shaftesbury Homes that took in pauper children and trained them to become seamen. Lord Shaftesbury was also responsible for procuring better housing for the poor of London. In Parliament he was instrumental in seeking to pass the Mines and Collieries Act, 1842, an Act that precluded women and boys under the age of thirteen years from working down coal mines.'

'You're not trying to kid us children were working down the pits, are you, Terry?' questioned Charlie, with a smirk on his face.

'No, I'm not trying to kid you about anything, you bird-brained, uneducated ninny. Didn't those nuns at the Catholic school you attended teach you any social history?'

'Of course they did. I know about Henry VIII's Act of Supremacy and his dissolution of the English monasteries,' replied Charlie.

'Oh! And did the nuns teach you about those ninety-five theses – the indulgences and the other rackets that the so-called traitors to the Catholic Church, such as Martin Luther, objected to?' Terry asked.

'Who?' replied Charlie, with a puzzled look on his face.

'Never mind,' replied Terry. 'Let that shallow birdbrain of yours go back to its dormancy. I don't suppose they even bothered to tell you about the Statute of Mortmain, passed by Edward I, that forbade the acquisition of land in England by ecclesiastical corporations without royal consent.'

'No,' replied Charlie, whose mental faculty had been dimmed by the torrent of religious brainwashing it had been subjected to during his long-distant school days, and which still held sway over logical argument and plain common sense. He sat silent while the grey cells of his now tormented mind tried hard to rationalise Terry's diatribe.

'Can you get back to the bit about children working down coal mines, Terry?' said Brains.

'Yes, of course,' Terry replied, 'but I'd better finish my discourse on Lord Shaftesbury first. He was also instrumental in bringing in the Factory Acts of 1867 and 1878. These were Acts that extended those of 1802 (proposed by Robert Owen and passed by the government under William Pitt) and 1819, which were specifically directed against unhealthy conditions in cotton mills and the abuses of child labour. Shaftesbury extended those Acts to cover all personnel in factories. However, they only covered working conditions. Wage payment was never written into any Factory Act. Children were a major source of labour in all mines and in other trades; and not just in coal mines as some history books would have us believe. They worked in tin mines, lead mines, iron ore and copper mines. They were also used as chimney sweeps, and were so-called apprentices in the factories and wool and cotton mills of the industrial revolution, and on farms doing all sorts of manual labour. But it was the coalmines that attracted Lord Shaftesbury's attention, mostly because of the serious accidents that continually occurred to children working in them. In the Stockbridge area, as early as the 1760s, the labour force working in the deep mine pits is recorded as having been predominantly made up of child labour. Lord Shaftesbury's government brought in mines and collieries legislation simply to put an end to the wicked, cheap and dangerous practices used by the mine owners, and based on children's and women's sweated labour.'

It was at this point that Charlie's voice broke in on Terry's discourse. 'Joe! Henry! The dunnage lorries are on the quay. George, there's been a change of plan. The heavy lifts haven't arrived in the docks yet, but there is a lighter of KDCs [knocked down case cars] that you can use to block off the square of the hatch. While you're getting the dunnage aboard the ship and laying it out over the cement, I'll get the lighter man to bring his craft alongside the quay and take off the tarpaulin covers. It's only five o'clock, so you've got a couple of hours till knocking off time.'

'Right ho,' George replied, then turning to Terry he said, 'You can give that tongue of yours a rest now; it must be running hot from its exertions. Get down below and unhook the dunnage when it comes down, and take the rest of these layabouts down there with you. I'm going ashore to take a look at those cases of KDCs, and to see if we'll have enough headroom if we stow them round the inner edge of the combing in the lower hold, to get the export cars under the lower 'tween deck ceiling.'

'Right,' Terry replied. 'We'll dunnage out the two wings first, then we can make a start on the cargo. As soon as you've landed the sets of dunnage to break out the first case of KDCs, Henry, we can start loading them as we work our way along the lower hold laying out the dunnage. By the way, we'll need a Port Authority quay gang tomorrow to bring the general cargo out of the transit shed, for filling in behind the KDCs.'

'Yes, I hadn't forgotten about that,' George replied as he disappeared through the deck hatchway.

When the sets of wood dunnage had been lifted off the lorries and put aboard the ship, I picked up the steel lifting wires from the quay and put them down into the lighter that contained the KDCs. It was less than five minutes before the barge hands had revved (wrapped up) the first case, I had lifted it out of the craft and deposited it in the hold to wait for Old Joe's signal before lowering it into place, hard up against the lower deck port-side combing. Before we had knocked off work for the evening at seven o'clock and replaced the beams and hatch covers, we had emptied the lighter of its KDCs and the lower hold was prepared for back-filling with general cargo first thing in the morning, with the runners (unprotected motor vehicles) to follow. Then, as I left the crane cabin and was making my way down the vertical steel ladders, I heard Terry call out, 'Is anyone coming to Smokey Joe's tonight for a drink?'

There was no reply from any of us; we'd had enough for one day. Our bodies needed sustenance, and our brains had absorbed about all we could take of his lecture for one day. So as all the best children's stories end, like good boys – and to save ourselves from another night of ear-splitting nagging – we all went home to tea.

*****

On the following morning, with an eight man Port Authority quay gang working out of the transit shed with general cargo, the wings of the ship's lower hold were in-filled out to the stringer boards, then motor vehicles were brought out one by one, which I lifted down into the ship's lower hold, where they were over stowed on the KDCs; after which two more loads of dunnage were hoisted into the lower hold to lay over the cement bags ready to take the heavy lifts. It was a job that took up all morning till we went to lunch. When we arrived back at work at 1 p.m. the lighter of heavy lifts had arrived and was tied up on the outside of the ship on her port side and the lascar crew had broken out two twenty ton ship's derricks. A pro-rata winch driver had been picked up to help me in the use of a union purchase, and, as I was the crane driver to the gang, I took over the up-and-down winch, being ready to lift the first heavy tractors aboard the ship and down into the square of the lower hold by 1.15 p.m.

It took the rest of the afternoon and part of the evening to load the heavy lift vehicles, and by the time we had finished putting the last tractor aboard we hardly had time to replace the beams and hatches on the lower hold and rig up the dolly brook before 7 p.m. Once again, Terry invited us to join him in Smokey Joe's for a beer. Except for Brains, Sandy and Charlie and me, all declined the invitation.

When we arrived at Smokey Joe's, Mary, Joe's most senior girl, was behind the illicit bar in the back room. Mary was one of those girls whose age can only be guessed at. She was tall, thin, had red hair, hardly any bosom and lashings of make up; in fact her face always looked as though it had a foundation of cement rendering that had been over-painted with whitewash. She always wore a deep red lipstick that matched her hair colouring, and she had a habit of continually pursing her lips, turning her head into her shoulder, then stroking her hair with her hand before butterflying her eyelids. From her physical appearance she looked as if she might once have been a marathon runner, but her caustic tongue betrayed her to be nothing more these days than an ageing old tart, a vindictive shrew. For some unexplainable reason she was the apple of Smokey Joe's eye: quite possibly an apple off the tree Eve got Adam to eat from.

When we arrived at the bar Mary greeted us with, 'What do you scruffs want?'

'A pint of beer each.'

'Don't you ever say please?'

'I didn't know this was one of those sort of places.'

'What sort of places are you talking about?'

'Cultural, you know what I mean, an edification institution.'

Mary pursed her lips, frowned, turned her head into her shoulder, ran her hand along the side of her hair, butterflied her eyelids, then she said, 'Mind your mouth. Rosie told me about you, you're one of those know-alls.'

Terry smiled and said, 'I hadn't realised my fame had spread as far as Smokey Joe's café. How much is the beer?'

'I'll pay for yours, Terry,' said Sandy, 'otherwise we'll never get served.' Then he turned to Mary and told her, 'I'll have enough of my old woman's lip when I get home tonight, so cut out the caustic, get on with your job and serve the beer, and leave us in peace.' With a pursing of the lips, a turn of the head into the shoulder, the stroking of her hair with her hand and a butterflying of the eyelids, she did. As Sandy left the bar he said to Mary, 'One of these days you'll flutter those eyelids of yours once too often, and take off.'

Mary turned her nose up in the air and said to Brains, 'What a horrible man.'

To which Brains was sensible enough to reply, 'I know, I work with him.'

As Sandy approached Terry, who had parked himself on a bench in the far corner of the bar, he threw a thumb over his shoulder and said, 'Fancy being married to a surly, coarse-mouthed bitch like that,' at which Charlie lowered his eyes and looked at his beer, while Terry just shrugged his broad shoulders. 'Not you too. It's no wonder you're never in a rush to go home.'

'Where did we get to, Charlie?' said Terry, before Sandy

had a chance to make a few remarks about the loss of their authority to 'her back home'.

'You were telling us about children and women working as sweated labourers down coal mines, and about Lord Shaftesbury's Mines and Collieries Act that brought an end to that practice, and also the Factory Acts that were passed to improve working conditions in the cotton mills and factories.'

'Well done,' said Terry, 'at least something is adhering to the few grey cells that are hidden in that thick cranium of yours, that's those that haven't been imbued with religious claptrap by those nuns.'

'Leave religion out of this. That was an accident of birth. Now get on and do what you're always telling us to do: give us the facts or at least the facts as you interpret them.'

'Right, if you're ready,' replied Terry. 'Now for the next session.'

3

The Gullible One

'Before you go on, tell us a bit more about William Wilberforce, because I've always been under the impression he was the key to the abolition of slavery,' said Sandy.

'Well,' said Terry, 'it's all a matter of interpretation really. I've already explained to you about the forerunners of the anti-slavery movement – Granville Sharp, for example, who blotted his copybook in my opinion when he shipped women from Wapping out to Sierra Leone with freed slaves. Then there was James Ramsay, John Newton, and Charles Kingsley who wrote 'The Last Buccaneer' – all three of whom were clergymen of the Church of England. And of course there was Charles Fox, a Radical Whig politician who was among the front rank of the anti-slavery campaign in the House of Commons, but who died before the Abolition of Slavery legislation was passed. So you see, Wilberforce, who was an evangelical Christian and a close friend of the prime minister, William Pitt the Younger (whom he had met when they were students at John's College, Cambridge), came some years after those other anti-slavery protagonists. There was also another chap whose name you never hear, a dedicated abolitionist by the name of Thomas Clarkson. It was through Clarkson that Wilberforce, a member of parliament for eighteen years, annually introduced anti-

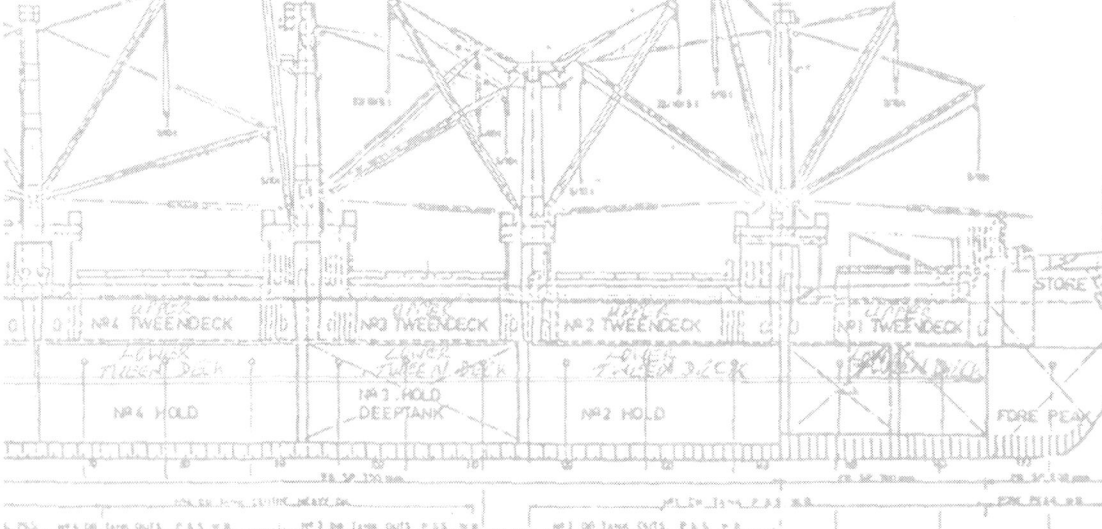

slavery motions before members of the House of Commons. Does that answer your question?'

'No. Not really. I can't understand why they were so keen on abolishing slavery. After all, they came from the class that depended entirely on other people doing everything for them. I mean the royal family even had lackeys whose only job was to wipe the king's arse,' Sandy replied.

'Yes,' said Terry, 'that was true in the middle ages, certainly when Henry VIII reigned. But I suppose that was because of his girth as much as his kingship; he obviously couldn't reach his own backside. However, I've always been of the opinion that the upper classes began to understand that bound slaves were a liability, in so far as they had to be purchased, fed, clothed and supervised till they died. On the other hand, wage earners could be taken on by employers, paid a paltry wage for their services, and worked long hours for six days a week. When they got sick and old they could be discarded at a whim.'

'Just like we are when we finish a job here in the docks,' I said.

Then Brains asked, 'Why did they only work six days a week, Terry? We have to work every day of the week, including Sundays, when there's ships working in the docks.'

'The answer to that question, Brains,' Terry replied, 'is church leaders were against Sunday working those days, with certain exceptions. Sunday came to be called the 'Lord's Observance Day', after an Act of Parliament in 1677. You see, Sunday was the first day of the week, supposedly set aside as a day of rest. But many churches were built within the great estates of the landed gentry in those days, and the bible-punching holy men were often sons of the lords of the manors. It was on Sundays too that the clergymen of the Church of England, and Holy Fathers of the Church of Rome within the estates of aristocrats and the landed gentry, and preachers at Presbyterian and Nonconformist churches in the towns and cities, got to work with brainwashing biblical texts, taken mainly from James I's authorised version of Jewish history. The estate's impoverished, down at heel, uneducated, ignorant bumpkin parishioners were threatened with thunderbolts or other devices sent by God. The poor sods were threatened too (and still are in some places) with fire and brimstone by courtesy of the devil who, clerics raved, would take them down into the fiery infernos of hell if they didn't obey the lawful commands of their lords and masters. Of course there was a second reason other than brainwashing for the Sunday sermons. The local bumpkins had to put a financial contribution from their paltry wages on the collection plate. Do you know, there was even a hymn sung in churches that went, "Bless the squire and his relations, And keep the poor in their proper stations."'

'Was that before coaching and railway stations were invented?' Charlie said jokingly.

Terry shook his head and went quiet for a few moments before he replied, then he said, 'Repeat the fifteen decades of Aves, you simpleton. Then fifty Hail Marys.'

'How do you know about that?' Charlie almost snarled.

'Because you are a sanctimonious numbskull,' replied Terry. 'It's obvious all those school days you shared with bluestocking nuns didn't do your limited mental faculty a lot of good. So why don't you just run your fingers along the beads of your rosary and do what the nuns spent most of their time trying to teach you? You've obviously forgotten that I attended the same Catholic school as you in the East End.'

'You did what!'

'Never mind, just let me get on with answering Brains' questions or we'll be here all night. Now Brains, my old friend, you have another question?'

'Yes. If we have Sunday observance, why do some people call it the Sabbath?'

'Through ignorance. Because the Sabbath day is the seventh day of the week, and is a Jewish day of religious rest. It's said that God created the world in six days and he rested on the seventh – the Sabbath. That's why Jewish people rest and fast on what we call Saturday.'

'Oh! I see,' exclaimed Brains, as he half closed his eyes and scratched the top of his head.

'Talking about religion – Holy Moses,' yelled Charlie. 'It's eight o'clock and I promised to take *her* to the Catholic church to play bingo at nine o'clock. I've got to go.' He stood up, swallowed the last of his beer and dashed out through Smokey Joe's back door as though the devil himself was chasing him.

'We might as well break up and go home,' said Terry. 'We're in the lower 'tween deck tomorrow.' And without another word we parted company to make our separate ways to the unkempt council houses we called home.

*****

At eight o'clock the following morning our gang slowly climbed the ship's gangway, and came together on the ship's deck. A lighter-man already had a cement craft alongside the ship stripped of its hatches, and he was waiting for me to remove the lighter's beams. So while the ship's gang were removing the tarpaulins from the hatches, and the wooden hatch covers, I lowered the crane's hook onto the quay, picked up the set of twos and the cement nets, luffed out to the lighter and placed the cement nets in the lighter's bay, lifted the lighter's beams onto the deck, then swung the crane's jib back aboard the ship to pick up the 'beam legs' to remove the ship's beams. By the time the down-holders had got down into the lower 'tween deck I had a set of cement hanging over the deck, waiting for Old Joe's signal to take it down into the hold.

The first sets of cement were always used to make a landing bed on which the following sets were lowered. The sets had to be placed exactly right, or when the following loads were lowered onto them these landing beds would collapse, and time and energy would be wasted in replacing them. We had got off to a flying start, and by 'Beer Ho' at 9.30 a.m. we had discharged 100 tons out of the first lighter. While we were having our tea break another lighter was brought under plumb, and made ready for us when we restarted work.

The use of cement nets, as opposed to cement boards, had radically increased the tonnages that could be achieved during loading operations. When cement boards were used it was difficult to achieve a loading tonnage of 260 to 300 tons a day. However, cement nets over 400 tons had become the norm by the mid-1950s, and in future years over 500 tons from 8 a.m. to 7 p.m. each day became the norm. It should also be remembered that barge hands loaded 500 tons onto cement nets, and the down-holders stowed 500 tons. In other words, between the barge hands and the down-holders 1,000 tons of cement were handled, but they were paid only for the 500 tons loaded and stowed aboard the ship. It should also be recorded that in the 1960s Captain Magnus Work DSC with Two Bars, Governor of the West African Terminal Stevedoring Company that serviced the ships of the West Coast Conference Lines in Tilbury Docks, became so concerned by the effect the massive tonnage output was having on his dock workers that he ordered his ship workers to limit working on cement to an eight hour day, from 8 a.m. till 5 p.m.; the two hours from 5 p.m. till 7 p.m. were to be worked on general cargo.

It was 9.50 a.m. before we got back to work. Old Joe had pulled his lemonade bottle filled with tea up on deck – with its three spoons full of sugar added – and after having drunk it he lowered the bottle back down into the hold for Brains to rinse and re-stow in the tea-box. I, on the other hand, had my tea and sandwich in the 'tween deck with the ship's gang, but returned to the crane cabin to remove the lighter's beams and put the cement nets on top of the cement stowage. The barge hands had come ashore and had made their way into the cement-carrying craft, and were ready for the next session of humping and thumping bags of cement into cement nets to take us up to lunchtime.

By 11.45 a.m. we had emptied the second craft of its 100 tons of hot grey torment and the port and starboard wings of the ship had been filled to a depth of eight bags. It now only left the fore and aft ends and the square of the hatch to be filled. This was a doddle of a job for the down-holders: we knew we could finish loading the 'tween deck by this evening, if the weather would hold fine for the afternoon. We had already loaded 200 tons during the four hours of the morning work period, and had six hours to play with in the afternoon. We kept our fingers crossed.

By the time the ship's gang had arrived back aboard, and the last of their heads and shoulders had disappeared down below the ship's deck hatch into the lower 'tween, I had lifted the cement nets into the already uncovered lighter, removed the craft's beams onto its deck, and had the crane hooks dangling over the first set of cement.

George had wisely sent Albert and Duffy, two of his down-holders, into the craft to make up a third team of barge hands, so I found myself working out of the fore and aft sections of the lighter. I was helped by the fact the craft was between the quay and the ship, close up to the dummy, so I set up a steady rhythm of working one, two, three along the craft. It took roughly two minutes to take a set of thirty-two hundredweight of cement from the craft into the ship's hold and to take an empty net back into the craft. That gave the barge hands six minutes to get a set loaded ready for me to remove into the ship, and the two corners of down-holders three minutes to empty a set, but as they were stowing the cement underfoot they had no trouble in keeping up with the barge hands. By 2.30 p.m., when Brains called 'Beer Ho', we had loaded forty-five tons from the craft into the ship. From 2.45 p.m. till 4.45 p.m. we loaded another ninety-six tons.

Each 'Beer Ho' time was much the same, except during the evening break at about 4.45 p.m. when I stayed in the crane cabin, and Brains provided my tea in the lemonade bottle.

We had one and a half hours to go before knocking off time, with fifty-nine tons required to finish the 400 tons of cement listed by the loading officer on his ship's loading plan; it (thirty-seven sets) was to go into the lower 'tween deck. We finally completed the job at 6.30 p.m. and walked off down the gangway at 6.45 p.m., after having replaced the steel deck beams, closed up the wooden deck slab hatch-covers and replaced the tarpaulins. There would be no discussion at Smokey Joe's café this evening – it was time to go home, wash or bathe, re-fuel and sleep.

We had never achieved such a high tonnage before, but we were neither pleased nor displeased with our efforts, just tired. In fact we never gave our achievement much thought. There was no kissing and hugging and running up and down the ship's deck shouting 'We are the Champions' and squirting bottles of champagne at each other (or in our case it would have been bottles of lemonade). To us it was just another day's work, one more day in what would be, as Terry, our intellectual, university educated, socialist, trade unionist workmate, told us, would be 'a lifetime of similar sweated drudgery that will continue till you are too old to carry on. Then it will be the scrap heap for the lot of you.' And he had continued, 'Had we been classed as athletes, for our achievement on this day we would have had our names brandished around the globe by the press and other media, supporting our miraculous feat of physical endurance, determination, will-power and courage. George,' he said, 'would no doubt receive a knighthood, Henry would have got a CBE, Old Joe an OBE and some of us others, us blokes who did the real work, would get an MBE. One or two of us might even have received the freedom of our towns – but the only reward any of us is ever likely to receive is much of the same donkey work we accomplished today, and this shall be for the rest of our working lives. In the national media we shall be ostracised; anti-worker resentment and other adverse publicity shall be all we can expect from press barons and their major share-holders, such as entrepreneurial industrialists, investment bankers, employment agency operators and others with a vested interest in manipulating truthful facts into media fiction. It will be government and media propaganda designed to engender in the minds of the general public a hatred and contempt specifically aimed at particular branches of blue collar workers: coal miners, dockers and railway workers in particular, us who are the precursors of the means of production. But it will be aimed surreptitiously, too, at all manufacturing workers such as vehicle assembly line workers and woollen and cotton mill operatives; the workers who actually manufacture and create the nation's wealth. Believe me, there will be no accolades given to the likes of us by those people who produce nothing of value but live off our skills and sweated labour, and cling to us like mistletoe on an apple tree.'

George, now looking forward to his promotion as a ship worker, had butted in, 'If you think it's so bloody marvellous in Russia, why don't you clear off and live there?'

Terry just laughed at him and replied, 'You've been

reading those right wing Tory propaganda news rags again, George. What you should be reading is the social and economic history of your own country. But of course you're getting ready for your next interview with the governor, aren't you? So you've got to get ready for a bit of fellow worker bashing. Talking about propaganda, George, it's a method of brain washing set up by a committee of cardinals in medieval times. Their intention was to control the minds of natives around foreign missions, but more specifically dunderheads like you, people who are unable to separate truth from fiction. By the way, I'm sure that Germany's Dr Goebbels, Hitler's propaganda minister, learned most of his propaganda techniques from the British national press and radio. After all, the Germans certainly learned how to set up concentration camps from those put in place by the British Army in South Africa, during the Boer War of 1899 to 1902, in which thousands of women and children died of hunger and disease.'

'Rubbish,' George replied. 'We British wouldn't do such a terrible thing.'

'As I've just said, you're gullible. If you read in the press or heard on the radio that people like you have intelligence, you'd be stupid enough to believe it. You don't think the governor's offering you a ship workers job because of your intelligence, do you?' said Terry.

'Well, he's not promoting me because I'm stupid, is he?'

'No! He's promoting you because you're a bloody yes man, and will carry out orders regardless of the consequences. Don't you think he's seen your army record, Sergeant Major – we all know your type, George. "I look up to them 'cause they're officers and gentlemen, but I look down on them 'cause them is privates and working class," sneered Terry.

'Actually,' said George, not rising to Terry's baiting, 'I didn't look up to them because they were officers, but because they had a higher rank than me. I looked down on the other ranks below me because I had three stripes and a crown on my arm and they didn't,' he said pointing at his shirt sleeve.

'Is that right?' said Terry. 'Now, where was I? Oh yes!

Now, if we had been in Russia and achieved this remarkable tonnage we would without doubt be in the vanguard of a Moscow May Day parade. We'd be seen flying a pennant that read "Four hundred tons loaded aboard a ship in one working day"; or words to that effect. We would all have had our names published in *Pravda*, the state newspaper, and our names would have been published throughout the Soviet states. We might even have been hailed as Heroes of the Soviet Union. However, for you, my compatriots, tomorrow will always be a wait and see day – a "wait and see what the morrow will bring". But whatever happens, believe you me, it shall be more of the same tomorrow as it was today, for the rest of your miserable wage slave lives. There's one thing you can be sure of, that unlike athletes not one of you will ever receive an honour or award for your contribution to the economic benefit of our employer, the national coffers or the glorification of the shipping industry. No, it will be our employers themselves, hell bent on receiving accolades, with the aid of the national media that support those wage slave drivers, who will see to that. In fact, except for us, the OST clerk, the ship worker, the tonnage clerk and the pay clerk (who incidentally failed to register an hour's stoppage time that would have reduced our day's pay by three and eleven pence half penny per man, if I hadn't checked the tick note), no one will ever know of our stupendous deeds, except the governor of course, who will pat George on the back at his ship worker's interview, before telling him of his good luck in being promoted to roughly the equivalent rank he held before being demobilised from the king's army as a regimental sergeant major. So, get yer 'air cut and stand by your 'ooks, you 'orrible lot, when George gets made up.'

George refused to be drawn into a slanging match by Terry's taunts, and he was quick to point out later that 'Terry was wrong about his prophesy of more of the same tomorrow. Because it was the day after that we had to load the other 300 tons of cement in the upper 'tween deck.'

The day following our completing of the 'tween deck cement cargo, we arrived back on the ship. She was getting low in the water now, only a few feet off her salt water plimsoll line. There were two lorry loads of rough cut wooden dunnage waiting on the quay, timber that was to be used to lay over the cement in the lower 'tween deck. Just inside the shed door a Port Authority quay gang was waiting on us to start work. They were old men in their fifties, sixties and seventies, tough old veterans of wars and dock work, men who could be relied on to do whatever was necessary to aid us in the ship loading operations we would begin as soon as the ship's gang had uncovered the deck hatches and I had done my first job, to remove the deck beams and slab hatches.

The barge hands now took on a different function. Two of them went aboard the ship and became down-holders; the other two became pitch hands on the quay, whose function was to secure all cargoes that left the quay for stowage in the ship. Their first job was my second, that was to hoist the wood dunnage off the lorries and lower it onto the sacks of cement in the lower 'tween deck, where the down holders would lay it over the bags of cement ready for the 'runners' (cars) to be garaged during the ship's voyage to the Far East.

George had received orders from Charlie, our ship worker, who had himself received orders from the ship's charge clerk, passed on to him from the ship's loading officer, to fill both port and starboard wings with runners, but to leave the hatch square open for some open-backed lorries. The reason for this was twofold: the lorries would fit under the beams in the square of the ship's hatch, and before the hatch was covered up the backs of the lorries could be filled with case work and topped up with light cartons between the beams. It was obvious, therefore, we would be spending the whole day completing the loading and stowage of the lower 'tween deck. It was a slow job which entailed the quay gang pushing the runners from where they had been parked, the open storage area between the transit sheds, out onto the quay into a lifting cradle under my crane, ready for me to hoist them into the ship's hold.

When we had completed the job of loading the runners, we then had to wait on a Port Authority tractor driver to tow the open-backed lorries under the plumb of the crane's jib on the quay. As it was near lunchtime – it was 11.40 a.m. – we stopped work and made our way to the bottom canteen, a dilapidated nineteenth-century public house that had been built when the docks were first opened. It sold beer of dubious strength, sandwiches of questionable origin and content, and tea and coffee that you could stand a spoon up in before sugar was added – it was a brew known among dockers and lighter-men, who did their best to avoid that venue if they possibly could, as Dead Sea Tea or Coffee, Paint Stripper Extract or Stewed Up Brew, for obvious reasons.

We had an hour or more to while away before we returned to work, so we made our individual purchases of the limited choice of sandwiches on offer at the bar, and bought a pint of what was presented as beer, tea or coffee. Actually all three beverages had the same look and texture: the beer was dearer, but the tea and coffee were stronger. When we had been served we congregated round a battered old wooden table that had obviously been part of the original furniture of the place. It was surrounded by cast-iron supported wooden benches where Terry had parked his bulky frame, and sat sipping his pint of beer while reading the *Daily Worker*.

At first we were silent, except for the sounds of beer sipping and sandwich chewing (only God could have known which breed of animal had been responsible for producing the leather that was in the meat sandwiches, if it was meat), but after having gnawed our way through the various door-step sandwiches we had been served the talk began to edge towards the subject of 'this week's pay' – and it wasn't long before Brains again raised the question of wage slavery with Terry,

'When are you going to finish telling us how wage slavery came about?'

Terry, obviously bored with the discussion that had been taking place, looked up from his *Daily Worker* and asked, 'Where was I before I was so rudely interrupted?'

'You were telling us how we would be treated like heroes if we were in Russia, because we had loaded 400 tons of cement in one day,' Sandy reminded him.

And Brains chipped in, 'You also mentioned the adverse propaganda put about by the media, propaganda that was always against the working classes, and that Goebbels quite possibly learnt how to use propaganda techniques from the British press and radio.'

'Yes, thank you for that, Brains, but I must press on. I have explained to you about the movement of repression from slavery to serfdom down to wages. Now I come to the ultimate means of repression used by one small section of the human race that has gained the capability to enslave the rest of us, originally by force of arms but now by primary physical needs, which are classified by industrial psychologists as food, sex, safety and shelter. We are what they in the man-management racket describe as blue collar workers, or units of production, although we should more accurately be referred to as black collar workers, on account of the filthy state we get in while we are producing the goods, services and wealth those in the establishment, the so-called upper class, and even the jumped-up middle class, all enjoy at our expense. I use the word "enslave" in its broadest context, that is the majority of a population within any industrialised country, simply because those workers have a limited opportunity to be anything other than factory fodder in peace-time, and machine gun fodder in war-time.'

'Why, in your opinion, is that, Terry?' I asked.

'Education,' Terry replied, 'or, to be more precise, a lack of it.'

'What's education got to do with it?' said Sandy sarcastically.

'It's got everything to do with it. Without education you are what you are, a manual worker who has the respect of nobody, and whose skills and abilities are recognised by nobody. If you complain or go on strike about pay and conditions of employment about your lot, you are ostracised, denigrated, openly and blatantly attacked by the so-called free press as "a bloody minded stevedore, docker, coal miner or factory worker" or whatever, and sacked from your job.

Even other members of the working class, who have no idea of your or their own true worth to society, verbally abuse you and each other among themselves: industrial workers who in fact are themselves, because of their lack of education, trapped in father to son, mother to daughter subservience. There is no way you can hit back at those parasites that live off of your sweat, except through collective unionism. They hold all the cards because they own all the means for anti-blue collar propaganda. You have no recourse to establishing a legitimate claim to social or economic justice, no matter how clever you may think you are, not because you don't have the mental faculty or intelligence, but because you have been deprived of the key that can set you free.'

'So what is the key and where do we find it?' Charlie asked.

'The key is access to education. Education can be obtained from schools, colleges and universities where there are teachers and lecturers. Without education you are as nothing within any society. The Chinese have a proverb, which is, "Genius without education is as unmined silver." All of you members of the proletarian class should reflect on the wisdom of that proverb, and see your children get the best education they possibly can to free themselves from the stigma of ignorance and the bondage of entrepreneurially imposed wage slavery, the manacles by which industrialists and merchants bound first you then, in the course of time, them, to the grindstone of wage slavery, as surely as serfdom was the chains that bound your fore-fathers to the lords of the manor.'

'But we've got schools and further education colleges where children can learn now,' said Sandy.

'Oh yes,' replied Terry, 'but how many of you have encouraged your children to use those facilities? How many of your children go to grammar schools, or have gone on to further higher education?'

There was total silence till Terry said, 'None! I wonder why?'

'Well, what's so important about education? We don't need it,' said Charlie.

'That's my point,' replied Terry. 'That's why you're a docker; that's why most of you were private soldiers when you were in the army; that's why you will grow old and impoverished; all that because you lack education.'

'Balls,' Charlie replied. 'You're educated, you've been to university, and you're a docker.'

Terry thumped his head into his hands, folded his arms, shook his head from side to side as if in disbelief, and sat looking at them before he replied. 'None of you get the message, do you? I'm a docker for reasons of my own. Unlike you I don't have to be, and I can choose my own time in taking up a lucrative post among colleagues in a profession. You lot are dockers because you have had no choice in the matter. Your fathers' occupations chose the level of your education, not your intelligence or mental capability. All of you would have been placed in the lowest classes of the schools you attended, with strict masters who taught you nothing that was of any value when you left school at fourteen years of age, except Old Joe, that is, who left when he was twelve. The whole social system works against you, the proletariat members of the population, for political and social reasons that are beyond the layman's ability to fathom out. But when you sit down and begin to analyse the cause and effect of Britain's rise from humble beginning to become an empire, it's then you start to understand it was the industrial revolution that not only created vast wealth for those who invented and owned the means of production, but it also created poverty and brought about disease and early death on a scale unknown since the fourteenth-century Black Death for the miners, dockers, factory and mill workers who really create the wealth of the nation.'

'How did that happen, Terry?' Brains asked.

'Quite simply because most of the factory, cotton mill, coal mine and quarry owners were too busy greedily making money, building flash houses for their wives and mistresses, and generally trying to outdo one another in their dash to obtain titles. Incidentally, it was an action replay of the antics of those sugarcane field and cotton plantation slave owners of the sixteenth and seventeenth centuries. Those workers who created the wealth, men, women and children, worked long hours without a break, lived in atrociously dilapidated houses, sometimes with families of as many as twelve in a couple of rooms, without access to clean water or sanitation, and died in their thousands, of dysentery, diphtheria, tuberculosis, scarlet fever, smallpox, asbestosis or other diseases, or from malnutrition, or from injuries caused by industrial accidents. The infant mortality rate was horrendous. The life span of working-class people was between seventeen years in some areas and thirty to forty years in most of the others. Country areas were an exception.'

'Is that why you became a communist, Terry?' Charlie asked.

'I'm not a communist, Charlie. I'm a socialist trade unionist,' Terry replied.

George looked at Terry, shook his head, looked at his watch and said,

'Holy Christ, it's five minutes to one o'clock, let's get back to work.' As George got up to leave so too did his not too happy band of merry men, who followed him slowly but silently back to the ship, with Terry and Brains lagging behind the vanguard, and Old Joe bringing up the rear, rocking from side to side as he swung his arthritic knees backwards and forwards like a couple of pendulums off old grandfather clocks.

4

Mr Sid

On reaching the quayside, we found the dummy that had been between the ship and quay had been removed. The ship was now lying beside the quay, resting against large tyre fenders. The ship's gangway had been re-sited; it now hovered about six inches above the edge of the quayside. The lascar deck crew, under the professional direction of the ship's serang (a crew member acting as a bosun), had 'broken out' the ship's twenty ton derricks, with the starboard derrick plumbing the centre of the crane tracks and the port derrick plumbing the centre of the open hatch.

A pro-rata winch driver had been 'picked up' in the Dock Labour Compound as my assistant on the over-side winch. He was a 'B' man, Sid ('Mr Sid to you, sonny,' he'd growled). Mr Sid was in his seventies or eighties, old enough to be my grandfather – perhaps even older – who knew more about driving cranes, winches, loading or discharging ships than I ever would. He had started work in the docks at the age of twelve when sailing ships were still in vogue, before Old Joe had been born I don't doubt.

We hadn't expected the ship would be beside the quay, though I should have known the five ton crane I had been driving during the morning would not be capable of lifting the heavy lorries that weighed between ten and twelve tons

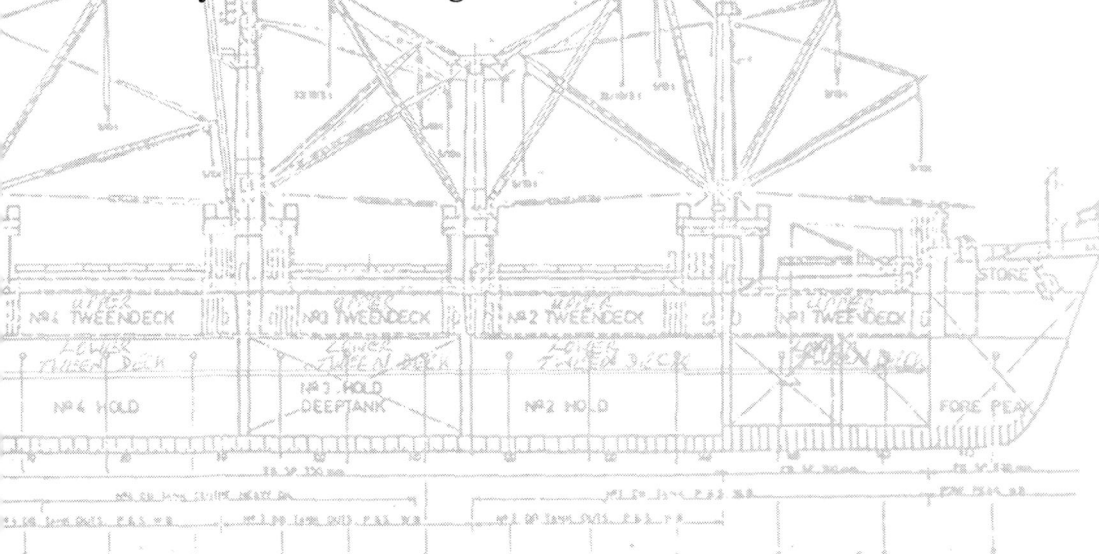

each. Therefore, on reaching the ship we went our separate ways.

The two pitch-hands stayed on the quay, preparing the vehicle heavy lift equipment that had been brought from the company's gear store. I made my way to check that the derricks, guys and lazy guys were properly secured to the appropriate cleats on the ship's deck, and in the correct positions. George had led his gang of down-holders slowly up the ship's gangway, from where they one by one disappeared from my view, down through the deck hatchway into the lower 'tween deck, to prepare for the arrival of the first lorry.

It was some minutes after we had arrived back aboard the ship that the tractor appeared drawing two heavy open-backed lorries, each of which had one of our Port Authority ship's-side aged gang in the driver's seat. Old Joe gave the signal to lower the 'union purchase' to pick up the lifting gear that was between the transit shed and the base of the crane, so the tractor could pull the lorries directly onto the lifting apparatus. This operation continued till the square of the lower 'tween deck hatch was filled with heavy lorries. It was then that George went ashore to select cargo to stow round the lorries and to fill the open backs. The serang was called out to get the lascar deck crew to re-ship the derricks. The Port Authority quay gang began to wheelbarrow loads of George's selected general cargo out of the transit shed and place it on cargo loading boards, after it had been measured and recorded by the OST clerks. (There were always two clerks to a ship's loading gang, one to measure each item of freight and the other to record the measurements, marks, numbers and stowage in the ship's holds.) I had gone ashore to climb up into the crane cabin ready to lift the sets of general cargo into the ship's hold. Sid was paid off and given his Dock Labour Board attendance book, stamped till 7 p.m.

First there came sets of cartons of Osram lamps that were to be stowed round the outside and between each vehicle; and these were followed by heavy casework that was loaded into the open backs of each lorry. Then, when that job had been completed (it took all the rest of the afternoon and evening), I re-shipped the upper 'tween deck steel beams and sister beams; and the ship's gang replaced the wooden deck hatch boards, which they then covered with a 'save-all', a tarpaulin hatch cover designed to stop any dirt or cement cargo from spilling down onto the freight in the deck below. By the time we had replaced the deck beams and hatches it was 6.30 p.m. Time to go home and recuperate, so as to be ready for the 300 tons of cement that was destined to be stowed in the upper 'tween deck on the morrow.

As it turned out, some of the gang made an intentional detour that took them to Smokey Joe's café, where they intended to quench their thirst with a pint or two of Joe's famous duty free, full strength, lukewarm beer.

Once again Rosie was behind the bar, her large half-exposed breasts resting on the counter. She greeted them with, 'What do you want tonight? We're not going to get another lecture on slaves and serfs are we? Because if we are I'm going to put ear plugs in.'

'You'd be far better employed tucking those dumplings of yours back in your bra,' said Sandy. 'It's no wonder women like you get raped.'

Rosie smiled, then replied, 'Joe don't mind his girls getting raped, as long as the rapist pays up, and if they don't pay up, Joe will see they are paid, as you well know.'

Terry butted in with, 'May I have a pint of Uncle Joe's?'

'Yes, I know Mr Know-all, ice-cold, lukewarm beer. You lot look nice and clean tonight. Been to a party, have you?'

'Stop taking the urine,' Terry told her, 'we've been loading runners and lorries today.'

'Runners, eh? So you'll be in the money next week.' Then Rosie winked at Terry and said, 'Shall I make an appointment for Thursday evening, say about 8 p.m.?' (Registered Port Workers were paid on Thursdays.)

Sandy broke into their conversation with, 'Is that when you want the rest of us to come back for our beer? Get a bloody move on, Rosie, or you'll have five dead bodies lying here on the floor by Joe's counter. How would he explain that to the police?'

Rosie winked, smiled, tapped the side of her nose and replied, 'Joe has his ways.'

So it was that Brains, Sandy, Charlie, Albert, Duffy and I

got served and were finally able one by one to follow Terry to the end bench, where we sat silently sipping our beer, waiting for someone to open the conversation.

Finally Brains asked, 'Why don't you get on with explaining about slaves, serfs and wage slave cultures?'

'How far did I get?'

'You was talking about greedy wage slave employers, poorly paid workers who lived in hovels that lacked proper sanitation or adequate water supplies, and about young pauper children from workhouses being used virtually as slave labour, and about workers dying by the thousands of all sorts of diseases and industrial injuries, and about the infant mortality rate being horrendous,' Charlie reminded him.

'Ah yes,' said Terry, 'the poverty-stricken, destitute, down-trodden, uneducated illiterate working class. My God, however was it allowed to come about that people were better clothed, better fed and generally better looked after as slaves and serfs than they were as free men?'

'How did it come about, Terry?' Duffy asked, while scratching his head.

'Well,' Terry said, 'in my opinion it all began with the Black Death of 1348–9, when a third of the population of England was wiped out by the bubonic plague, because it was that one single incident in our social history that did away with serfdom and brought in the era of wage payments for craftsmen and labourers.'

'So what you are saying is that wage payments are an evil?' I suggested.

'Yes I am, unless they have certain safeguards. Before serfdom declined and wages became the normal practice for settling payments between employer and employee, there was a chronic labour shortage. Then, at the behest of the manorial lords, the government introduced wage control by passing the Statute of Labourers Act in 1351. That legislation was reinforced by the Poor Laws Act of 1388, which was not only an attempt to fix wages but also to prevent mobility of labour, which would cause wages to rise, thereby stifling the economic conditions that encouraged craftsmen and labourers to 'tramp about' the countryside searching for the highest paid employments.'

'About the same as it is here in the docks today,' said Albert, 'where we wander around the Dock Labour Compound asking ship workers what cargoes the ships they are working are carrying, or, if there are no ships here in the docks, being directed to work in other docks or other ports by the Dock Labour Board manager, or sent home on fall back pay.'

'Yes, that's exactly right,' replied Terry. 'Seven hundred years after an Act was passed to stop workmen wandering about the country seeking employment that paid the highest possible wage, the Labour government in 1947 introduced the Dock Workers (Regulation of Employment) Act onto the statute book, an Act that took from ship owners the responsibility of directly employing dock workers. This was achieved by setting up an employment agency, namely the National Dock Labour Board, an organisation that, when there are no ships in the docks, operates to the detriment of those peripatetic dock workers that the Act created.'

'Cut out that communist propaganda, Terry,' Charlie said, 'I don't believe a word of it!' This brought a burst of laughter from the rest of the eager listeners.

'What don't you believe?' said Duffy. 'All that Terry has told us about the conditions we work under is absolutely true. We live and work under those conditions every day, or haven't you noticed? Ignore that idiot, Terry, and get on with it.'

Terry smiled and continued, 'What I'm trying to explain to you is how governments and employers work in unison to manipulate working conditions to suit employers' needs. This is achieved by specific groups of people, who wish to move, in this case, employment away from slavery to a wage-based system. Now just supposing William Wilberforce and his cronies had an ulterior motive for abolishing the slave trade. Suppose it wasn't a humanitarian act at all, but was based on the fact that since the breakdown of the manorial system, paying wages had proved to be more profitable to the employing classes than serfdom. For as I've already explained to you, slaves had to be captured or purchased from tribal chiefs, clothed, fed and housed. If slaves had a family, the slave owner had to provide for them, too. But wage earners, on the other hand, had to house, clothe and feed themselves and their families. Now I've always been a sceptic where do-gooders are concerned. I've always tried to analyse the motives behind their actions. It's my considered opinion that some if not all of the people behind the motion for the abolition of the slave trade had a vested interest in creating a pool of cheap labour, so-called free citizens for whom they had no responsibility outside the workplace, and took very little or no responsibility for what happened to their employees. That was why Robert Owen, with the aid of William Pitt the Younger, forced the first Factory Act of 1802 onto the statute books.'

'Why do you think Owen and Pitt did that, Terry?' Brains asked.

'Robert Owen knew from experience that atrocious working conditions were totally unnecessary in mills and factories. He had proved his point by experimentations in employment, housing and the education of child workers at his New Lanark Mill. On the other hand, I've not the slightest idea what William Pitt's motive was, except that what Robert Owen was practising, and advocating in economic and social policy, was simply plain common sense. As I think I told you earlier, my old friend,' said Terry benignly, 'the Factory Acts were directed chiefly against the unhealthy conditions in coal mines, cotton mills and factories; and the gross and glaring abuses of so-called child apprentices sent to work in those industries by the Poor Law commissioners from parish workhouses, mostly from the south of England.'

Rosie, who had been listening to Terry's diatribe from behind the bar, asked, 'What were workhouses, Terry?'

'Rosie, my lovely innocent lass, they were institutions that had been set in place after the introduction onto the statute book of the Poor Law (Amendment) Act, 1834. Until then the Poor Law was administered in England under a system that dated back to 1601, when overseers of the poor were established for each parish within the realm. In 1834 the system was overhauled and boards of guardians were set up. The object of that exercise, as far as I can make out, was to remove beggars from the streets, many of whom were servicemen wounded during the Napoleonic Wars and their wives and children who had little or no means of supporting themselves. The unemployed, too, suffered the same fate and were incarcerated in those hell-holes that were the poor man's Black Holes of Calcutta. You just don't know how fortunate it is for you and us that workhouses were abolished by the post-war Labour government, when the Poor Law (Amendment) Act was replaced by the National Assistance Act of 1948 – but only after there had been a separating of the non-disabled unemployed through the Unemployed Assistance Act of 1934, and the removal of the responsibility for destitute kith and kin from relatives through the Pensions and Determination of Needs Act of 1943.'

'Oh! Well I never,' said Rosie squinting and furrowing her brows, obviously perplexed by Terry's explanation.

'That's all well and fine, but why did the government build workhouses, Terry?' said Duffy.

'There were in my humble opinion two reasons behind their introduction. The first was to get beggars off the streets, as I've just said, and the second was to punish those working-class people who were unable to work or to find work and earn wages, or to be more specific, the lack of the means to obtain any form of wage income.'

'So who were they?' Duffy queried.

'As I've just explained to you, people too old or disabled to work, the feeble minded, single or widowed women with children who were unable to financially support themselves, orphaned children, ex-service men suffering from war wounds (they couldn't become Chelsea Pensioners if they were incapacitated in any way), the industrially injured, workers unable to return to work because of their injuries.'

'Holy Christ, Terry,' said Albert, 'these days the workhouses would be full of injured miners and dockers.'

'Yes, they were then, and their families too if the wives couldn't work to keep them,' Terry replied.

'Who were the people responsible for creating those inhuman conditions, Terry?' said Duffy.

'I've already told you, the ruling class of aristocratic landowners who sat in the House of Lords, and the puppet politicians, most of whom came from aristocratic landowning families, and who were elected in what were known as rotten boroughs. Those were the people who sat in the House of Commons and made and passed the laws of the land to the benefit of middle-class merchants and factory owning entrepreneurs, who imposed long hours of work, intolerable working conditions and low pay on their employees. Ship owners, too, who sent thousands of merchant seamen to their deaths in "coffin ships". These were the people whose only interest lay in the profits they could extract from their various enterprises. These were the tyrants who caused the wage-earning poor to become so destitute in old age and infirmity that they were obliged by the law of the land to become incarcerated in workhouses.'

'You're giving us a load of cods, Terry,' said Charlie. 'I for one don't believe a single word of it.'

'Of course you're right, Charlie,' replied Terry. 'No one could believe that such diabolical conditions ever existed in what was reckoned to be an enlightened society – that one class of citizens could impose such intolerable conditions on other citizens of their country. What you're implying, though, is that when Albert told us earlier on that his grandfather died in a workhouse he was lying.'

'Are you calling me a liar, Charlie?' said Albert, ''cause if you are you'd better step outside.'

'Hold on you two,' said Duffy, 'there's no need for that sort of talk. We all know Charlie was brought up in a convent. That's why he's got those girlish ways.'

'What do you mean by that?' replied Charlie.

'You sometimes talk out of your fanny, you ignorant idiot.'

Suddenly Joe appeared on the scene, summoned by Rosie pressing the secret alarm bell that rang in his office. 'Got a problem have you, lads?' he said, squinting down his nose and wringing his hands together. 'It's about time you all went home to bye-byes, isn't it? Working on that black P&O cement job, aren't yer? Go off home and get a good night's sleep and I'll see you again tomorrow night.'

We knew Joe wasn't making a suggestion or a request. He was giving us an order. So without any more ado and a 'good night Rosie' as we walked past her, we left Smokey

Joe's smoke-laden bar by the back door, and walked out into the cold but refreshing night air.

*****

The following morning at eight o'clock we were all gathered on the quay. For some reason unbeknown to us, the ship's gangway had been raised and the ship's gangs were unable to board the vessel. Not to be deterred, George told me to climb up into the crane cabin while he and the lads got hold of a set of fours (four hooks attached by spliced wires to a single steel ring) and a cargo board (about six feet by eight feet), which they laid flat on the quay. Then, having placed the hooks one on each corner of the cargo board, all six of the ship's down-holders, and Old Joe the hatchway-man, got on the cargo board, which I then lifted up onto the ship's starboard deck. They were soon busily stripping off the tarpaulin hatch covers and wooden hatch boards so I could remove the ship's steel beams and slab hatches. Their obvious reason for getting to work was that they were piece workers, which was the next step down from being classed as self employed.

In the meantime, while the gang were stripping the covers off the deck hatch boards, I had slewed the crane ashore, picked up the cement nets and had them dangling over a now partially open lighter's cargo bays of hot bags of cement. The barge hands were already aboard the lighter, helping the lighter-man to remove the hatch covers, and after removing the cement nets from the set of twos they were soon creating a halo of grey cement dust as they thumped bag after bag of cement down onto the nets.

While the barge hands were busily filling the cement nets, I slewed the crane jib back over the ship's hold and removed the steel hatch beams. Then, to my surprise, while the ship's gang were placing the last of the wooden slab hatch covers, Old Joe beckoned towards the cargo board I had last seen leaning against the ship's deck rail on which there had been placed a plain wooden box. I slewed the crane round, Old Joe attached the set of fours to the crane hook, I brought the crane's jib back over the cargo board, two members of the ship's gang placed the set of four hooks on the lifting rings of the cargo board, and I slewed the crane back over the quay – where a black hearse was parked between the crane tracks. The vehicle's driver indicated for me to slew the cargo board up behind the rear door of his vehicle, and a coffin was quickly and unceremoniously slid into the back of the hearse. It suddenly struck me, the only time we working-class people get to ride in a posh car is when we're dead. I couldn't help but smile to myself while thinking that at least it's something worth looking forward to.

As soon as the hearse had been driven off along the quay, the lascar deck crew, under the ever vigilant eye of the serang, lowered the ship's gangway. Almost as soon as the gangway had been made secure, men were pouring up it to begin work. Very soon there was the inevitable whining of electric winches, the cracking of guy and lazy guy wires, and the ghostly silent apparitions that were sets of cargo, which left the quay, Thames barges or steel lighters to disappear into the wide open mouths of the ever hungry ship's holds. The skills to be seen during the cargo loading operations were sheer magic.

Before we had began work, George had asked Terry how many sets of thirty-two bags there were in 300 tons, and been told 190. George calculated that, given each craft held eighty tons, taking into account the time lost when changing over from one craft to another, the average set would take about three minutes. However, Terry pointed out that if we worked each craft up till our meal break, the empty craft could be shunted out and a fully loaded craft brought under plumb. That way, he had explained, we'd lose no time and we should be able to discharge one craft of eighty tons before our tea break and one craft of eighty tons before lunch. Terry had also explained to George that eighty tons of cement represented 1,600 bags, which at thirty-two bags to the set equalled fifty sets in each craft. So it was that at 8.15 a.m. we began loading the 'grey torment'. The job went so well that by 9.30 a.m. Brains had made the tea, the first craft had been discharged, the barge hands had come aboard and I had come down out of my crane cabin to join the rest of the gang in the upper 'tween deck, where they were slowly sipping at mugs of hot brew, and gnawing away at sandwiches or bread rolls. Old Joe, who had hoisted his lemonade bottle filled with tea (with its three spoonfuls of sugar) up on deck, sat by himself on a wooden deck hatch on the port side of the ship, watching seagulls dipping their beaks into the dock water as they scavenged raucously and ravenously among flotsam and jetsam for scraps of food, in the filthy, oily, polluted water of the enclosed docks.

When we returned to work after 'Beer Ho' at 9.50 a.m., the second cement craft was already in position between the quay and the ship with its hatches stripped off. We were quickly back to work with a steady rhythm of sets coming first from the bow then the aft bays of the craft. The rest of the morning went off as well as the first session. We had emptied the second craft of its eighty tons of cement at 11.45 a.m., before we went off to lunch, and by the time I had replaced the lighter's beam the ship's gang were coming out of the deck hatch and walking down the gangway. I came down out of the crane and followed the silent, perspiring, tired and cement-covered gang members towards the only 'watering hole' within half a mile – the bottom canteen.

When we arrived at the canteen we joined a long queue of dockers, lighter-men and lorry drivers, all waiting patiently to be served with victuals of dubious origin, with beer or tea that had been brewed or stewed to the same texture and colour, from Flossie, one of the barmaids, whose prune-like wrinkled face gave me the impression she had been employed in that place since it was opened – almost a hundred years before.

Then, having been served with delicacies that could only be found in the bottom canteen (although similar samples might have existed in the British Museum), we found ourselves once again at the same old wooden scrubbed table, on the hard wooden benches we'd sat on before. We sat for some time in silence, eating and drinking. Terry, as was his way, sat aloof (but not apart) from the rest of us, deep in his private thoughts, reading that day's copy of the *Daily Worker*. He occasionally stroked his chin, scratched his head or took a swig from his mug of tea, or was it beer? While he was in this pensive mood, Brains said to him, 'Are you going to finish telling us about the slave, serf and wage slave cultures, Terry?'

'And about the rotten boroughs, Terry. What were they?' said Albert.

Terry turned round to face Brains and found he was looking along two lines of expectant faces, faces covered in grey cement dust – with only pairs of tired blue eyes and red rosy lips that had been washed clean by tea or beer to show he was not looking at two rows of stone statues.

'Ah, yes!' Terry began. 'Rotten boroughs. What were they? They were the instruments of a corrupt totalitarian state. Rotten boroughs were the means by which the aristocracy, lesser nobles and wealthy landowners had taken control of both parliament and the House of Lords after the English Civil War of 1642 to 1649. During the reign of Charles II the House of Lords took control of the running of the country, with its members selecting and electing their own kith and kin to Parliament, in order to serve their own interests.'

'How could they do that?' said Charlie. 'It's not possible in a parliamentary democracy.'

Terry burst out laughing, then continued, 'I don't know what those nuns put into those tiny grey cells you've got in your cranium, Charlie. But take it from me that history shows quite clearly that England wasn't a democracy then, no more than it is today – but I may come back to that point later. What I can tell you is that the aristocrats, they were war lords in every sense of the word, and those others of their ilk not only ruled the country, they also owned it and everything in it. It was by this means they were able to select and elect to parliament anyone they chose to represent them. That's where the aptly named rotten boroughs got their name, because they were owned outright by the landowning classes, and regardless of the numbers of inhabitants they sent two representatives each to parliament. However, things began to change under the influence of the Industrial Revolution, when the mill and factory owning entrepreneurs of the Midlands, and Northern English towns such as Birmingham, Manchester and Leeds, who had no parliamentary representation at all, began agitating for a plebiscite.'

'What's a plebiscite, Terry?' asked Brains.

'It's the means by which plebeians, that's us, the common people, like what we are in the eyes of the non-working, non-producing classes, are given the right to vote for a policy which they know is beneficial to them, but which cannot be carried out without plebeian support. Democracy is the exact opposite to what the English parliament had become. Under the aristocrats that had taken control of the House of so-called Commons, through their control of the House of Lords, democracy was defunct. Do you understand that?'

'Yes, I think so,' said Brains, slowly scratching his head.

'Right then,' Terry continued. 'Now as I've explained, the mill and factory owning entrepreneurs who had become rich, many exceedingly wealthy during the Industrial Revolution, now wanted some say in the running of government, and pressed for parliamentary reform. You can bet that there was opposition to such proposals from the ruling elite, who looked down their noses at those jumped-up underlings, whom they despised as tradesmen. But the dye was cast, and the first Reform Bill was passed in 1832.'

'A Reform Bill to reform what?' I asked.

'Nothing really,' Terry replied. 'It was just a ploy to placate the newly wealthy emerging middle classes, except that most of the rotten boroughs were deprived of their parliamentary representation. But as far as the ordinary working-class citizen was concerned, nothing had changed. This was because suffrage (the right to vote) was only given to citizens in towns who owned or rented houses worth ten pounds a year, and to renters and owners of land of a certain value in the countryside. In this way those people who became known as the middle classes, lawyers, doctors, mill and factory owning entrepreneurs and such like, were given the right to vote; but ordinary working-class people such as mill and factory workers, colliers and coal miners, and agricultural workers, anyone who produced the goods and services the upper and middle classes depended on for their sustenance and welfare, were still excluded from the franchise.'

'What's a franchise, Terry?' Brains enquired.

'It's more or less like a plebiscite, except it gives certain citizens the right to vote in the election of their representative to a governing body, as opposed to a single unilateral vote on some specific policy.' Terry then looked at his watch and said, 'Come on, you plebeians, it's 12.50, time for your next medication.'

'What's that?' Duffy said in complete surprise. 'What medication?'

'A good old dose of hard work, my boy. Wasn't it Winston Spencer Churchill who once said, 'A dose of hard work never killed anyone?'.

'How the hell would he have known that? He never did any hard work in his life,' Albert said.

Terry waved his finger in a joking but menacing way at Albert. Then he said, 'Don't forget Winston built a wall round his country shack, Chartwell.'

Albert replied, to everyone's surprise, 'Then it's a bloody good job he didn't live in China, weren't it?'

After that comment we all got up to leave. All of us, that is, except George, who had sloped off when we left the ship, to join the ship workers in their so-named *Adobe Hacienda,* at the far end of the Southern Quay, no doubt in order to pick up a few tips on how to bully and brow-beat men in civilian occupations. He'd no doubt been an expert at imposing 'strict disciplinary procedures' when he was a sergeant major during the war. But as Charlie had said, 'It's obvious he'd been a right bastard in the army, otherwise how would he have risen to sergeant major from the ranks?' It was a comment that brought more than a few groans from the 'old sweats', those former soldiers who were survivors of battles fought by King George's British Expeditionary Forces in Belgium and France before they had been evacuated from Dunkirk, and who had then been sent to join the Imperial Army in North Africa, the 8th and 5th Armies in Sicily and Italy, and the 14th Army in the jungles of Burma. In fact, wherever British troops had fought the king's enemies, those scruffy, unwashed, cement-caked veterans had seen service under sergeants and sergeant majors like George. By the time we had walked slowly and silently back to the ship, and climbed up the gangway onto the ship's deck, that momentary hatred of all military personnel with stripes on their arms, pips or crowns on their shoulders or gold braid hat-bands, had disappeared as we prepared to face a much worse enemy than the bitter memories of their military service for king and country. Physical fatigue.

5

George's Antecedents

When we arrived back at the ship George was already on board waiting for us. He was leaning over the ship's taffrail, talking to a lighter-man on the next but one craft we were about to discharge. He turned away and came along the deck to tell the down-holders, Old Joe and me the news. 'It's been decided not to split the marks in the next two craft. We're going to discharge two full lighters of cement, 160 tons instead of the 140 tons that were originally allocated to our hold. How many sets is that, Terry?' he asked.

Terry looked at George through squinting eyes, with something of a scowl on his otherwise smiling face, before he answered. 'A bloody fine ship worker you're going to turn out to be. Isn't it about time you began to work these simple sums out for yourself? It's quite simple really. There's twenty hundredweight to the ton, therefore you multiply the eighty tons in the craft by two, then you add two noughts, which equals 1,600 bags in a lighter. You then multiply that number again by two, which equals 3,200 bags. Have you got that so far?'

'Yes, I think so,' George replied.

The next thing you do is to divide 3,200 by thirty-two, which is the number of bags of torment in one set. Thirty-two sets into 3,200 gives you exactly 100 sets. To get an

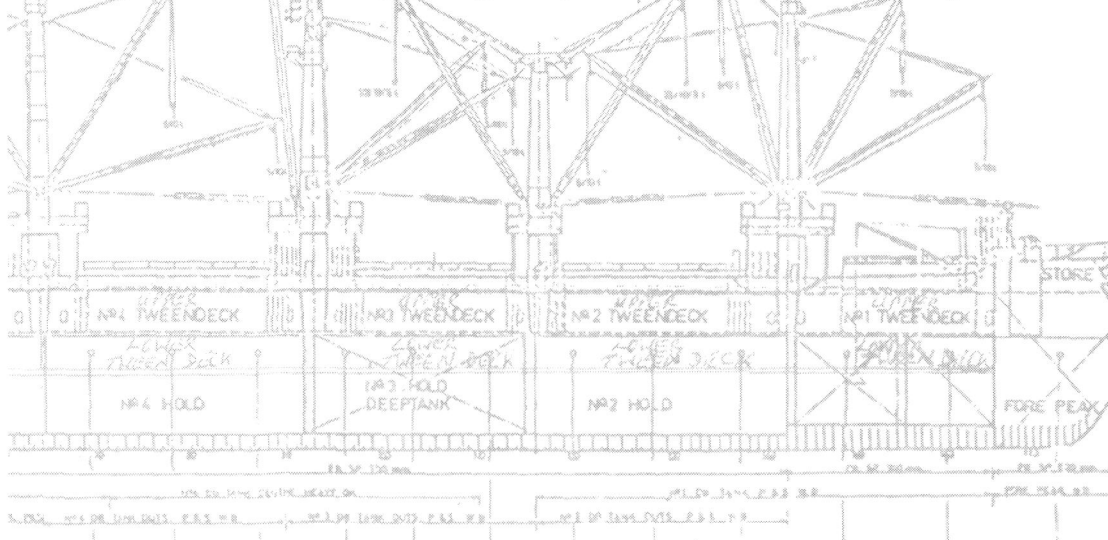

approximate time to finish discharging the first craft, you simply multiply fifty sets of thirty-two by two minutes a set, which equals 100 minutes. That calculation means we should finish emptying the first craft by 2.30. Now you have to add on twenty minutes for our tea break. That means we should start on the second craft at 2.50 and another ten minutes before the first set comes out of the second lighter, let's say by three o'clock. There's sure to be other stoppages, but we should finish discharging the second lighter by approximately five o'clock this evening, or as an academic economist might say, "all things being equal",' Terry informed George.

'Then we'd better make the job go till after five o'clock. We can spend from 5 p.m. till it's time to knock off flooring out the timber dunnage over the cement. We'll be over-stowing the cement with general cargo tomorrow, so we must finish loading this cement by tonight, right,' said George.

*****

I went ashore with the barge hands and climbed up the three levels of steel ladders into the crane cabin. The barge hands went directly onto the next loaded cement lighter and I picked up the cement nets from the quay, swung the crane's jib out over the lighter and lowered them down onto the top bags of cement, before removing the lighter's beams and putting them on its deck. We then began the task of discharging the cement from the lighter into the ship's upper 'tween deck, with a steady rhythm of thirty-two bags to a set. All was going extremely well, and we had almost completed discharging the craft, when there was a flash of lightning and a peal of thunder. When I looked up I could see black clouds had blanketed the north-eastern sky. I shouted down to Old Joe to get the dolly-brook rigged up. Two of the down-holders came up on deck to give him a hand as he ran the steel wire from a winch drum down from a derrick's head to be shackled onto the top of the dolly-brook. In the meantime I'd gone on removing sets of cement from the craft, had just finished its discharge and put on the beams when God (or it may have been the devil) decided in his infinite wisdom to send first hailstones, then rain, down in torrents.

Fortunately Old Joe and the down-holders had managed to rig the dolly-brook up in time to stop the rain getting on the cement cargo, and they and the barge hands who had come up onto the ship's deck, when they had finished discharging the lighter, had vanished down through the deck hatch into the 'tween deck, where Brains had returned with his teapot, and where, when I arrived on the scene, the whole gang were sitting round a table made up of wooden deck hatch boards, lighted by a cluster of electric lamps, slowly masticating sandwiches, bread pudding or cakes as they recuperated from their recent hard labours.

It was several minutes after I had arrived in the 'tween deck before anyone spoke. Of course it had to be George, as he had the greatest vested interest in what he was about to say. 'This rain's a bloody nuisance, isn't it?' he moaned. 'I wanted to get this cement loaded and finished with by this evening.'

'Yes,' replied Terry, 'so did the rest of us. It's only half past two, and if the rain stops before half past three we'll still have time to finish the job, George. Don't worry, the governor won't hold you responsible for this delay. It's simply an Act of God.'

'Stop having a go at George, Terry,' Albert said. 'Get on with telling us some more about the slaves, serfs and wage slave cultures.'

'Yes, Terry,' said Brains, 'go on, tell us more.'

'OK. Where did I get to? It was the abolition of the rotten boroughs under the Reform Bill of 1832, wasn't it?'

'Something like that,' said Charlie, 'although I don't see what that's got to do with anything.'

'You wouldn't,' Albert replied. 'Now keep your mouth shut and let Terry explain what the significance of the Reform Bill was.'

'It was quite simply,' replied Terry, 'a wedge that was driven into a corrupt system of national control, the first stage in establishing parliamentary democratisation, but it was a step that didn't come cheap.'

'In what way?' Duffy asked.

'Because our forefathers had to fight and die for it. You know yourselves that even today the only way we can redress our political grievances and show our revulsion at government policies is by marching en masse on Parliament, or when the next general election comes round by voting out those politicians we consider have failed in their duty to us while in office. But you have to remember, before 1832 not even those people with wealth who were not landed gentry had a political say in who should run this country.'

'Then who do you blame for that, Terry?' Brains asked.

'Oliver Cromwell, to some extent, although I don't suppose he realised what the consequence of his actions would be.'

'What on this earth did Cromwell have to do with it? Albert asked.

'He destroyed the Levellers movement. The Levellers were a political party with extreme Republican intention, led by a John Lilburne. They were prominent in England during the English Civil War, but Cromwell was responsible for stopping them from carrying out their professed objective of destroying all social and economic inequalities. He crushed the movement in 1649.'

'Why did he do that?' Albert asked. 'After all, the English Civil War was fought in order that parliament should rule the country by democratic consent, wasn't it?'

'Was it, indeed?' Terry replied. 'That may have been the original intention of those that fought for political reform, against King Charles I's crazy notion about the divine right of kings to rule as they thought fit. But unfortunately, all it did on Cromwell's death, and with the Restoration of the Monarchy, was to allow the Whigs, then the aristocrats through the House of Lords, as I've already explained to you, to take control over the House of Commons by the simple instrument of rotten boroughs and rigged election results.'

'Can you prove any of that guff?' said Charlie. 'I don't believe a word of it!'

'Why should you? Why should any of you believe a word of it? But let me tell you this, you had disbelieve it at your peril.'

'Why?' said Duffy, who had been lying on the hot bags of

cement in the shadows by the stringer boards near the ship's side, and who we thought was sound asleep.

'I'll tell you why!' exclaimed Terry. 'Because good men and women have died in order to change the political system to what it is today, while other men and women are constantly striving to turn it back to what it was previously; a class structured society of them and us, where them rules us, and us of the working class having no say in the manner by which we are politically controlled and economically treated.'

George, who had made only one previous contribution up to this stage, and that was just to moan about the rain, finally butted in with his second comment. 'Just like your communist mates in the Kremlin, no doubt.'

'Oh,' said Terry, 'it's nice to hear from you, George; you who once lived in the delightful back street hovels of the tenement slums of London's East End, down in Limehouse Causeway, or was it Wapping Steps, close to the river where the rats, bigger than the feral cats, scavenged along the foreshore, in the roadways and even in the hovels. Where mothers were afraid to leave their babies in case they should find they had been eaten alive, and where most of the dogs that ran wild among the back alleyways and warehouses probably knew that if the didn't run they too could find themselves being stewed up for dinner. You, George, soon to be elevated to the dizzy heights of ship worker, lived at the very heart of the opulence of crime, grime, prostitution, disease and the final indignity to a wage earner's life of drudgery and despair – death in a Poor Law Guardians' workhouse and burial in a shallow unmarked pauper's grave, in some dingy, unkempt churchyard attended only by the workhouse beadle. But he was there just to see the gravedigger didn't nick the corpse to flog it to the surgeons at St Thomas's or Guys Hospital. That was, of course, unless he was in on the scam; then he would turn a blind eye to the transaction.'

George said nothing more, but if looks could have killed Terry would have writhed in mortal agony till he died where he sat. But Terry's gaze back was more intense, and George was forced to avert his eyes as Terry's words brought back the memories of those dark days of George's childhood and youth, suffering the indignity of being referred to as a guttersnipe, mudlark or street Arab by those toffee-nosed bastards from up west, who on some auspicious occasions would drive their posh cars round the dock roads and watch with delight as he, and other children from poverty stricken waterside families, along with orphans and even destitute men and women, fought each other for the handful of copper coins they would throw into a previously silent, simmering, hostile crowd of onlookers. That was before the Second World War came to save him from the ravages of the poverty and degradation that had afflicted his family for generations – and the mention of the workhouse had brought back to him the bitter memories of his grandparents' last residence, before they had died and been buried as Terry had just said – in shallow paupers' graves. Terry's recitation on the ills of George's childhood had obviously struck its target. George got up and without another word, not even looking back, climbed out over the bags of cement and disappeared up through the deck hatch. As George retreated Terry softly sang, 'When George lived down in Wapping, beside the River Thames, Down among the hovels, and condemned tenements, He'd do a bit of mud larking, or begging by the door, Of the Old Prospect of Whitby, that nestled by the shore, Where his bruvver was a mugger, and his muvver was a whore.'

'OK, Terry,' said Duffy quickly, 'cut it out, George's gone.'

The silence that followed this interlude in the 'tween deck could only be likened to that in a submarine under depth-charge attack, as all the crew waited in anticipation for the next explosion. That is, silent except for the continuous pitter-patter of raindrops falling heavily onto the sailcloth canvas of the dolly-brook over our heads. Then Brains suddenly broke the silence by saying, 'Where were those people who died, Terry? Who killed them?'

'Well, the first of several places that springs to mind is Peterloo, in August 1819. What took place there was known as the Peterloo Massacre. Actually it was a meeting of operatives, ordinary working people, who were gathered in St Peter's Field, Manchester, with Orator Hunt, a radical politician, in the chair. They were assembled at a law-abiding meeting to demand parliamentary reform. But the local magistrates of Manchester got into a panic, describing the meeting as a riot, and ordered the dispersal of the crowd by Manchester yeomanry. The meeting ended with the deaths of a number of unarmed people and the wounding of several hundred others. It is on record that a Sir William Napier was sent north with an army larger than the British army that faced Napoleon at the battle of Waterloo, to suppress any further meetings. That's how much regard was given to the wealth-creating citizens' right to demonstrate. Of course, there was another factor in this tragedy that has never, to my knowledge, been examined by social historians.'

'What may that have been, Terry?' Duffy asked.

'Simply whether the magistrates who gave the order to disperse the crowd did so because they genuinely believed there was going to be a riot, or because they had a vested interest in breaking up the meeting.'

'In what way?' I asked.

'That they were local satanic mill owners (as the poet Blake may have put it) or wealthy landowners. This would have meant their reason for suppressing public meetings was more to do with possible demands by their workforce for wage increases than with keeping law and order by military force.'

'Why do you say that?' Duffy questioned.

'Because that's what happened in the case of the Tolpuddle Martyrs.'

'Who are they?' said Charlie. 'Another of your lot?'

'If you mean who were they, you ignoramus, they were six uneducated farm labourers from Dorset who were sentenced in 1834 to seven years' deportation to Australia, not for carrying out trade union activities, which is the reason usually given for their incarceration and deportation, but for administering what were termed to be illegal oaths. They were actually sentenced under a naval mutiny law, drafted after the Nore Naval Mutiny of 1797, when Royal Navy sailors led by Richard Parker, a press ganged teacher from Sheerness, I think, mutinied against the harsh conditions, poor food and pay and brutal punishments. At that time Royal Navy sailors hadn't had a pay rise since the sixteenth century. As for their being "another of my lot", I've no doubt that had they been alive today they would have been trade union socialists. However, the main reason for their harsh sentences is said to be that the government hoped punishments of such severity would prevent further working-class unrest.'

'And keep the poor in their proper station,' said Sandy.

'Exactly,' Terry replied.

'Did it?' Albert asked.

'No it didn't. In fact it only exacerbated an already delicate political situation. The Peterloo Massacre was still a focal point in the minds of radical thinkers. The sentences imposed on the Dorset labourers caused further working-class unrest, so much so that the government was forced to remit the sentences in 1836. But the reason for the Dorset labourers' deportations was the same as that for the slaughter of working-class people at Peterloo: the suppression of working-class rights, wages and conditions of employment. It was another nail in the coffin of a totalitarian ruling, high living, socially psychopathic, unsympathetic, unjust elite. But it had the effect of being another step towards parliamentary reform, another step towards . . .'

'Getting this bloody ship loaded,' yelled George's angry voice from the deck above. 'It's almost stopped raining and the lighter-man's stripping the hatches off the lighter, so get up here and give me a hand to lower this soddin' dolly-brook.'

Terry looked at his watch. 'It's half past four,' he informed us. 'We can still empty that second craft if we get a move on.' So we all quickly went our separate ways; the barge hands and I went ashore, they to the craft and me up into the crane cabin. Old Joe waited on the 'tween deck hatches for me to bring the crane jib over the ship and lift him up onto the deck, as he clung like a limpet to an empty cement net. Brains collected his teapot and made his way to the ship's galley to make a pot of tea. It would be a mug of tea to be drunk as we went on loading the cement. George, our erstwhile down-hold foreman, soon to be elevated to the dizzy heights, stood on deck by the open hatchway, seething with anger.

I lifted the first set of cement out of a Thames lighter

that was lying on the ship's port side out of my sight, and swung it inboard over the hatch. As I have explained, Old Joe had stopped in the 'tween deck, waiting for me to lift him up onto the main deck. Luckily George was on hand to direct me to the spot the down-holders had chosen to make their landing pitch. When the first set was landed Old Joe stepped onto an empty cement net that had been hooked onto the crane, and I lifted him up onto the port side of the ship where he would be working till we finished discharging the lighter and came ashore to begin loading general cargo.

George in the meantime had disappeared down through the deck hatch, to take charge of the loading operation. I have to admit this had slowed down, what with the rain and the animosity between George and Terry. It was obvious to me that Terry resented George's promotion, not through envy, I hasten to add, but because he was about to lose a workmate. The gang without George would, Terry knew, be like the proverbial ship without a rudder. That was till someone could be found with George's ship-loading skills – there was, he knew, no one in the gang capable of filling that job except himself, and Terry knew too that the labour contractor by whom we were employed would never stand for a socialist trade unionist being given the down-hold foreman's job. What is more, all the gang were aware of this. So they slowly carried on, taking some three minutes to unload each set. By my reckoning this meant we should have discharged the lighter at, but not before, 6.55; that would leave no time to cover the hatch up before we finished work. Damn it, I thought, and shouted down to Old Joe, 'Tell George we're falling behind time. We've only done twenty sets in the last hour.' With that bit of intelligence things changed, and we reduced our set handling time back to two minutes. We (or to be more precise they) finally finished loading the cement at 6.40, and after closing up the hatch the gang walked off the ship at 6.55, tired, hungry, covered from head to foot in grey cement dust – dust that had formed into small round grey balls because of the rain and sweat, and clung to their clothes, eyebrows, hair and the ends of their noses, giving the impression on first sight of baubles hanging on unfinished concrete statues.

Nothing was said as we began our half-mile walk or cycle ride to either the Riverside Passenger Terminal, to catch a ferryboat across the river to Gravesend, or to Tilbury Town. But it went without saying that the local men headed for Smokey Joe's, where we went directly through the front door and, after furtive glances in all directions (no police about), disappeared into the backroom unlicensed bar for a much cheaper pint of beer than we could get in the local public houses.

Mary, Joe's number one girl, was leaning over the bar, trying hard to expose what little she had in the way of a bosom. As we entered the room she straightened up, and as she did so we followed her every movement as she pursed her lips, turned her head into her shoulder, stroked the side of her red hair with her hand and butterflied her eyelids.

'Oh!' she exclaimed, 'all going a little quirky are you? If you want to take the piss I'll serve you with some.'

'Nothing's changed there then, Mary, that's what you usually do,' said Sandy. 'Either that, or the beer tastes like piss when you draw it up on the pump. That's what I like about this place of Joe's. Nothing changes from the beer down to the girls, and by the look of you, Mary, they don't change very often.'

With that comment Mary went through her usual rigmarole, turning her head into her shoulder, stroking her hair with what looked like chipolatas for fingers, and butterflying her eyelids till Smokey Joe came on the scene. He'd obviously been alerted by Mary pressing the alarm button.

'Got a problem have we, lads?' he said as he stood before them with a broad grin on his fat flabby face, and wrung his hands together while surveying them through half closed, squinting, black, piercing eyes.

'Not really, Joe,' said Sandy. 'Your Mary's not up to a bit of "dock humour", that's all. She's got a caustic tongue, and she's about as lively as a long dead gunfighter.'

'What do you mean by that?' said Joe.

'She's dead bloody slow on the draw, drawing up a pint that is! All we want is a drink.'

Joe picked up a pint glass from a shelf behind the bar,

half filled it from the bar pump, took some coins out of his pocket, rang them up on the till and began to have a drink, before saying, 'Serve the lads, Mary. Can't you see they've been working on cement all day?' Then, as was his custom, he said, 'Finished loading the upper-'tween deck with cement today, you have. You'll be on general cargo tomorrow, won't you. If you decide to come into my café after work tomorrow night make sure you don't come in that filthy state.' Then without saying another word he walked away and disappeared into his back room office.

Mary, with a smirk on her face that almost cracked the foundation of her make-up, and a snub of her nose as though she had won a great victory, drew up six pints of beer and plonked them one by one on the bar counter.

'Right, there's your beer,' she proclaimed, butterflying her eyelids. Then to her utter surprise and bewilderment, once again without any rehearsal, all six of us went through what were her usual antics by pursing our lips, turning our heads into our shoulders, stroking our hair with our fingers and butterflying our eyelids. Mary burst out crying and ran off into Smokey Joe's back room, quickly to be replaced by Rosie, whose first words were, 'Six pints, that'll be ten and a ha'penny each.'

Not another word was spoken as we, each having paid Rosie separately for his pint of beer, made our way to the usual corner of the room, where we sat in silent meditation for a few minutes, brooding over the supercilious attitude of Mary, Smokey Joe's personal female assistant – no doubt an assistant in more ways than one.

Then Sandy said, 'What happened after you finished telling us about the Dorset labourers being deported, Terry?'

'You've got a short memory, Sandy,' Terry replied. 'George called down the hatch for us to "get this bloody ship loaded", or words to that effect.'

'Ha-bloody-ha!' exclaimed Sandy. 'You know full well what I mean. Did it have any effect on the political scene, that's what I'm asking.'

'Well of course it did. It increased the tempo for change in many ways. Political reform was called for by an organisation called the Chartists, workers began to organise themselves through trade unions, and John Howard and Elizabeth Fry began the reform of an archaic prison system.'

'Tell us about all of them things,' said Brains.

'Well, I may as well start with prison reform. First you have to understand that incarceration in prison was as good as a death sentence, for once inside a nick a prisoner either died of starvation or what was known as prison fever – one of the numerous diseases associated with filth, lice, malnutrition and lack of any form of ventilation or sanitation. Prison reform was actually begun in the late eighteenth century by John Howard, a noted philanthropist. His experiences as a French prisoner of war roused him to attempt some reforms of the abuses of prison life. When he became the Sheriff of Bedfordshire he did a grand tour of the county jails of England, and the mass of information that he gathered was laid before the House of Commons in 1774. This brought about the first prison reforms.'

'So Elizabeth Fry wasn't the first prison reformer?' said Duffy.

'No, of course not.'

'Who was she, anyway?' I asked.

'She was the third daughter of a wealthy Quaker banker by the name of John Gurney. She was born in Norwich in 1780 and given a good education by her parents, then when she grew up and got married she devoted her life to prison reform and the reform of criminals – as well as other benevolent charitable enterprises. Elizabeth Fry died in 1845, but it wasn't till 1865 and 1898 that Prison Acts were passed to modify prison life and begin programmes for prisoner reform. I don't suppose for one minute she would have claimed to be the first prison reformer. She would have known of John Howard's dedication to prison reform and of the legislation on prison reform passed by the House of Commons. She just carried on with John Howard's work. But, as with the slave trade, the later reformers got the kudos that rightly should have gone to the pioneers who did most of the ground work.'

'You mean people such as William Wilberforce and Pitt the Younger got the kudos for the abolition of the slave trade,' said Brains.

'Absolutely right, my old friend,' Terry replied. 'But there's another crucial factor in this debate.'

'What's that?' Sandy questioned.

'There were two major prison reformers, John Howard and Elizabeth Fry, both from wealthy, upper-class backgrounds. As I said, John Howard had experience of incarceration in jail while a French prisoner of war. Elizabeth Fry, on the other hand, had had no such experience. But long after those two were dead, the wealthy upper or middle classes, with one major exception, didn't bother to look into, or change, the terrible conditions of those people working in mines, factories and cotton mills. These were the wage payment industries of the late fifteenth up to the twentieth centuries – industries that not only produced the goods and services that made this country the wealthiest in the world, but which through the lack of properly regulated wages for services rendered and hours worked also produced one of the most uneducated, poverty stricken, undernourished, poorly housed and downtrodden societies on this earth. In fact conditions were so bad in most industries that even callous government ministers were forced to take action, through legislation in the House of Commons. For example, Factory Acts, as I've already explained, first came onto the statute books in 1802 and 1819. They were directed chiefly against unhealthy conditions in cotton mills and the glaring abuses of child labour. Those Acts and others covering working conditions in every kind of industry were summarised in the Consolidating Acts of 1878 and 1901. Factory inspectors were employed to make sure that the Acts were put into practice, but they were too few in number to have any real effect on abuses that went on unchallenged in many districts for years, and in some industries still do to this day.'

'You said nobody from the wealthy middle classes, with one major exception, came to investigate. Who was he?' said Sandy.

'Actually it was a *she* by the name of Annie Besant, but I'll come to her later because of the major role she played in the formation of trade union policy as it related to "pacified industrial action". But I must first explain about other contrived abuses of workers.'

'What, for example?' Duffy asked.

'The truck system illustrates very well some employers' indifference to their employees.'

'What was the truck system?' Sandy inquired.

'It was the partial or entire payment in goods, as opposed to payment in money. It is recorded that it was common practice in the early days of the factory system to pay all or part of a worker's wages in inferior goods, goods the employees then had to sell on themselves to obtain an income. The truck system had been practised, as records show, for roughly 500 years before the first legislation was passed, the Truck Acts, which forbade employers from laying down conditions as to the way in which workmen should be paid.'

'When was the first Truck Act passed, Terry?' Duffy asked.

'The first act is recorded as having been placed on the statute book in 1464, specifically to protect workers employed in the woollen cloth industry. Another such act was passed in 1701 covering woollen, linen, fustian, cotton and iron manufacturing, and yet another one was passed in 1817 for workers employed in steel manufacturing. All the earlier Truck Acts were repealed by the Truck Act of 1831, which was itself superseded by the Truck Act (Amendment) Act of 1887 and the Truck Act 1896. But that's enough about that subject for the moment. What's next on the agenda?'

'Chartism,' replied Charlie, who had been sitting with his eyes closed, giving the impression he was asleep. (In fact he may have been for all the intelligence he ever showed on any subject.)

'Right!' said Terry, 'Chartism it is.'

'Not tonight it isn't,' said Rosie. 'It's time for you lot to get off home and to get yourselves cleaned up, watered and fed, before that cement you're all covered in sets. I don't want to have to ask Joe to call out his friend, the monumental stone mason, to come down here to chisel you all out of your concrete jackets. After all, he'd be more inclined to put you into a concrete jacket if Joe asked him to.'

Of course Rosie was right. She knew it. We knew it. But

we were far too proud to admit we were clapped out. So we drank up the last of our beer, pulled ourselves up onto our feet, and with a 'goodnight, Rosie' we sauntered past her and slipped one after the other through the back doorway of Smokey Joe's café, disappearing into a heavy mist that lay under a dark, moonless and starless sky, where the only sounds that could be heard were the deep blasts of ships' foghorns and the toot-toots of tugboats' sirens, somewhere out there on the deep dark sinister waters of a bleak, fog-shrouded river.

6

You Bird-brained Nincompoop

On the following morning at 8 a.m., with a heavy blanket of fog hanging over the river and docks, most members of the loading gang were assembled on the ship's deck. However, three of our number were missing: they were Gravesenders who, no doubt, were waiting patiently on the town pier, or vehicle landing stage, on the Kent side of the river, waiting on a ferry boat skipper to decide whether or when to take the risk of crossing the river with a ferryboat loaded down to the gunwales with frustrated passengers.

Aboard the ship some gang members were talking among themselves, while others were sitting on the wet, fog-dampened deck hatches, smoking pipes or hand-rolled cigarettes, waiting for George to turn up and tell them what that day's loading programme was to be.

Then Terry said, 'Let's get a section of the hatchway uncovered, then we can get down into the 'tween deck out of this soddin' fog. Brains, you go and make a pot of tea.'

It was quite odd really, looking back on it, that when Terry, just an ordinary member of our ship's gang and looked on as a communist agitator, gave out orders, everyone obeyed them without question; even though they often questioned (somewhat mutedly, I hasten to add) his purported political sympathies.

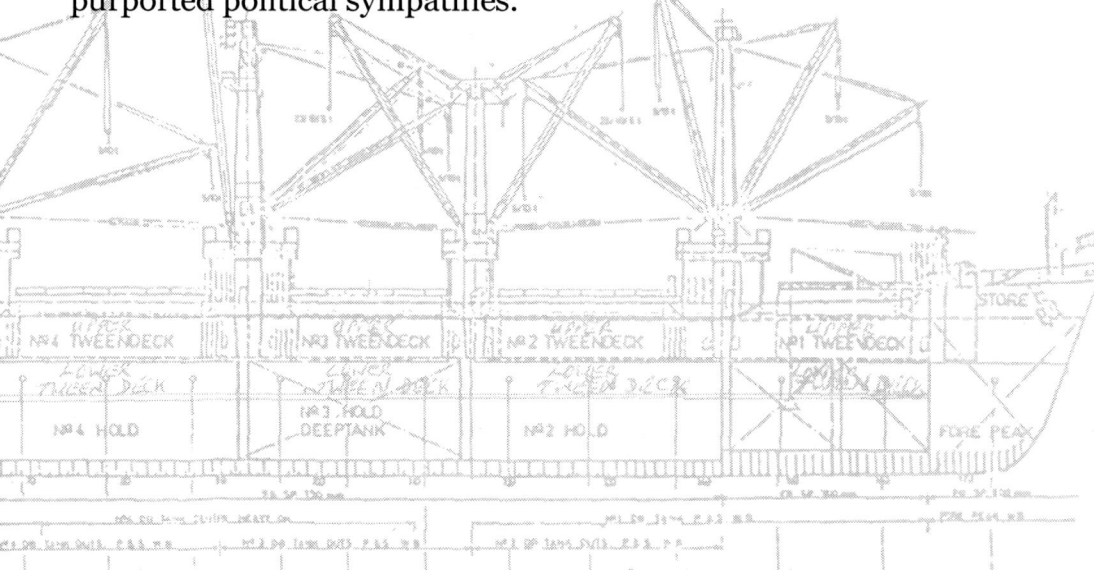

In consequence of his orders, the tarpaulins covering a section of the wooden slab hatch-boards were rolled back, a slab hatch-board section was removed, electric lamp clusters were run down into the upper 'tween deck to give the gang some extra light. Then we clambered down into a cargo hold that was still being heated by the cement cargo we had loaded on the previous days. Even Old Joe had decided to make the effort to join us in the warmth and comfort of the upper 'tween deck, to have the luxury of drinking his tea out of a (purloined) PLA mug, as opposed to swigging it out of a lemonade bottle, standing up on the exposed, cold, wet, open ship's deck.

Brains soon returned from the ship's galley with a large pot of tea, (tea filched from tea-chests on our last tea discharging job) to which he added a tin of Nestlé's creamy Carnation evaporated milk (said to have been purchased from a grocer's shop outside the docks) and half a pound of Tate and Lyle sugar (acquired during our last sugar loading job from a ship berthed at the Riverside Deep Water Jetty).

I was always amazed at the change in the morale of men when they had a mug of tea in their hands, and this occasion was no exception. As they chatted to one another, Terry had climbed up onto the warm bags of cement, and was sitting with his back to the stringer boards reading the *Daily Worker* when George climbed down into the 'tween deck.

'What's on, George?' Sandy asked.

'Nothing,' George replied. 'There's no local quay gangs available. The Dock Labour Board is sending for men from the Upper Docks. You can be sure they won't get down here till mid-morning, not at the rate of knots those steam trains travel on the Fenchurch Street to Southend line. We'll just have to amuse ourselves till they turn up. By the way, the Gravesenders are on their way down the quay. You'd better save them a mug of tea each, Brains.'

'Have those dunnage lorries turned up yet, George?' Terry asked him.

'I don't know. I'll go ashore to find out.' And without even bothering to have a mug of tea himself, George climbed up out through the deck booby-hatch, and we heard the sound of his boots as they quick-marched along the steel deck above our heads, the sound tailing off as he reached the ship's gangway.

Sandy said, 'You may as well get on telling us about the Chartist movement till we find out what's what, Terry.'

Terry closed his newspaper, slowly folding it and putting it into his coat pocket before speaking. 'Chartism was a political movement of the working classes of Britain, starting in the mid-nineteenth century in order to bring about a social change in attitude by the aristocratic and entrepreneurial classes towards the working classes; or what I prefer to call the wealth-producing classes. However, it was the Reform Bill of 1832 that gave into a movement that asked for a share in political power. Chartism found expression in a document called the People's Charter. This was more or less a demand by the literate, mainly self-educated working class for the introduction of a Bill of Rights for the benefit of the proletariat.'

'What would a Bill of Rights have achieved? Had there been other Bills of Rights?' said Duffy.

'Only one in Britain to my knowledge,' Terry replied, 'and that was embodied in the Declaration of Rights accepted by William and Mary in 1689.'

'What was the reason for that, then?' Albert asked.

'It set out the law under which William and Mary were to rule. It declared the abdication of James II. It also contained thirteen clauses relating to citizens' freedoms.'

'Such as what?' said Sandy.

'Such as the right of parliament to hold parliamentary elections. Also, the king was forbidden to make new laws or to neglect any old ones, his keeping of a standing army in peacetime was prohibited, as were stifling the freedom of speech, or refusing to receive petitions from his subjects. Nor was he to levy taxes or to levy excessive fines, and dispensing with or suspending laws made by parliament was also not allowed.'

'What effect did it have on ordinary people?' Old Joe asked.

'None,' said Terry, 'nor was it meant to apply to them, because if it had there would not have been any rotten boroughs or similar vote rigging and fiddling that went on between Whig and Tory grandees, for control of the House of Lords and the House of Commons. It could not have happened. What the Bill actually did was to take the previous powers of national policy control away from the royal prerogative, and place those powers in the hands of a corruptly elected House of Commons, and an even more corrupt, non-elected, self perpetuating (through privilege of birth) House of Lords. So you can see that both the lower and upper Houses had ceased to represent the nation at large. In fact they had become councils of aristocratic nobles and self-serving wealthy landlords, hell bent at all costs to preserve the privileges of power they had usurped from the Crown and the indigenous population.'

'In what way did they usurp power, Terry?' said Duffy.

'Well! They had already usurped the powers of the Crown under the Bill of Rights, and they continually denied the democratic rights of citizens to a franchise, which would have given them the right to vote in parliamentary elections. Therefore it was a matter of what they did with that power. Just as an example, while Charles Fox, the third son of Lord Holland and educated at Eton and Oxford University, William Wilberforce and their political cronies were beavering away at "freeing the slaves", members of the House of Commons were introducing new acts of repression on the population, through legislation known as the Speenhamland Act, which came into force in 1795. It was an Act that virtually made slaves of miners and factory and mill workers.'

'With what objective?' Albert asked.

'Historians say it was a political ruse to suck into the factory system all kinds of workers, which included the cheap labour of women and children, and after 1834 large numbers of paupers were sent from workhouses into what was nothing but factory slavery.'

'But what caused all the poverty?' said Sandy.

'Well,' Terry replied, 'it's been blamed on the agrarian revolution and the land enclosures that almost ran in tandem with the industrial revolution. Between them they transformed conditions in the countryside. This was based on the advances in farming techniques that took place because of the growing demand for cereals, meat and wool. The outcome of this, as I have already explained, was the passing of the Speenhamland Act, which was introduced as a war measure in 1795 and remained in force till the Poor Law Act of 1834 was passed. It has also now been recognised by historians that the main purpose of Speenhamland was to create a free labour market for factory-owning entrepreneurs.'

'Yes! Just like the Dock Labour Boards were set up under the Dock Workers (Regulation of Employment) Act for the benefit of a free labour market for the shipping industry employers,' Old Joe said.

'That's right,' replied Terry. 'But in the case of the Speenhamland Act, the object of the exercise was to create a free labour market by removing surplus populations from the country areas to the factory areas. So you see, it created pools of cheap labour at near starvation levels under the Speenhamland system of poor relief in what was termed a free labour market (which it was for the employers). By the way, to make sure government policy was carried through, parliament passed a number of repressive measures: the Aliens and Traitorous Correspondence Acts of 1773, the suspension in 1794 of the Habeas Corpus Act, the Treasonable Practices and Sedition Acts of 1776 to 1778, the Combination Acts of 1799 and the Corresponding Societies Act of 1800. In other words, a total repression of all rights and freedom for the Crown's subjects.'

'So, Terry, what did the Chartists want to happen?' enquired Duffy.

'What they actually wanted and proclaimed was a People's charter, drawn up in 1838 – a document that embraced six points.'

'What were they?' Old Joe asked.

'They were proposals that neither the Whigs or Tories could tolerate at that time, especially as they came from representatives of the wealth-producing classes.'

'Yes, we grasp that, Terry, but what were they?' said an angry Albert.

'They were manhood suffrage, which means the right to vote in elections; equal electoral districts, in other words no more rotten boroughs; the abolition of property qualifications in parliamentary representation; and the payment of members of parliament, all of which took the form of a petition presented to the House of Commons in 1839. The petition was said to have been signed by over one and a quarter million people and, surprise surprise, it was rejected by the House of Commons.'

'So what did the Chartists do then?' asked Duffy.

'They made preparations for another, much larger, petition to the House of Commons; a petition that it was claimed had six million names. The Chartist leaders were determined to overawe Parliament by a march on London, but this was thwarted by the dear old Duke of Wellington, the erstwhile commander of troops policing London.'

'Was that the same Duke of Wellington who won the Battle of Waterloo?' Duffy said.

'Yes and no,' Terry replied. 'Yes it was the same Duke, but no he didn't win the Battle of Waterloo. Let's put that statement in its true perspective. It was British and Allied troops under his command that won the Battle of Waterloo. It's the same sort of parlance that goes on with all the top people who get rewarded and feted for the achievements of others.'

'What do you mean?' said Old Joe. 'Like Christopher Wren, the architect who got all the accolades for building St Paul's Cathedral, but didn't lay a single stone?'

'Yes, Joe,' said Terry, 'and Horatio Nelson too, who got all the praise for winning the Battle of the Nile and the Battle of Trafalgar, where he was in fact lying on his back having been shot in the spine as the battle raged about him.'

'Was that when he is reputed to have said "Kiss me Hardy"?' said Duffy.

'Yes!' exclaimed Terry. 'But I'm sure he didn't say it.'

'Well, he said something like that, it's well documented,' Charlie butted in.

'What he really said, I'm sure,' replied Terry, was "Kismet, Hardy".'

'Kismet!' exclaimed Old Joe. 'What does that mean?'

'Destiny or a predetermined event, something that was bound to happen sooner or later, in other words Fate.'

'But he was the admiral in command of the British fleet

at Trafalgar,' said Duffy.

'Yes, and a great commander and tactician he was, too. But without his sailors he would have been like a pond without water, a jockey without a horse, a captain adrift without a crew. It's the way the people at the top, mostly so-called high born, appoint or nominate into responsible positions other wealthy individuals or toadies, in order to impress upon common people like us just how important or clever or brave they are, and how subordinate we of the lower classes are because we're unimportant and stupid, at least in their eyes, till there's work or fighting to be done. It's the very thing we're discussing now.'

'But Nelson was Britain's greatest admiral, wasn't he?'

'Not if you read about Oliver Cromwell's General at Sea, he wasn't.'

'Who on earth was the General at Sea?' I asked.

'He was a bloke by the name of Robert Blake who was born at Bridgewater in 1599. He was a successful soldier under the Commonwealth before Cromwell sent him to take command of the navy in pursuit of Prince Rupert and the Royalist fleet, which he destroyed. Then he beat the Dutch under Van Tromp, De Whitt and De Ruyter. He then took his fleet and sailed under the great guns of Tunis into the harbour, where he had his sailors set fire to a fleet of Turkish pirate ships that had for years been raiding the west coast of England and the east coast of Ireland, kidnapping people for slaves. But his final and greatest feat was the annihilation of a Spanish fleet in Santa Cruz Bay under the shadow of the Peak of Tenerife, a battle which was recorded as 'one of the fiercest actions ever fought on land or sea'. He died at sea but was brought home and buried in Westminster Abbey. But on the Restoration of the Monarchy his body was disinterred and thrown into a rubbish pit. So much for heroism if you're from the wrong class or your face doesn't fit.'

'Yes! We get that message, Terry, but get on with the story,' said Duffy, 'we haven't got all day.'

'Well, it's obvious that parliament upheld the Duke of Wellington's action by failing to countermand his orders to use military force against the Chartists. But in consequence all a corrupt parliament achieved by its connivance was to drive the Chartist movement underground. It didn't collapse as the political parties of those days assumed at the time, or historians have wrongly assumed since. The political philosophy of Chartism lay dormant while the perpetrators of the movement worked towards their political objective, which was a freely and democratically elected government. In other words it brought them time in which to resurrect their political ideology, an ideology that was later supported by the Wages Theory of none other than Karl Marx and Friedrich Engels.'

'What do you mean by dormant?' said Brains.

'They took time off to slumber, to sleep, no doubt while they slumbered perchance to dream; dream of a time when this "Land of Hope and Glory, Mother of the Free" would become a truly democratic nation and unburden itself of the miscreants who had the temerity to rule them without their authority. However, the petition's rejection, and the use of the military to stifle the freedom to demonstrate, gave rise to great political agitation throughout the country, a political agitation that was said to have been snuffed out after 1849 by the Duke of Wellington's military intervention, just as the Levellers movement for political reform had been snuffed out by none other than Oliver Cromwell two hundred years before, in 1649.'

'Now you're bringing your mate, Karl Marx into the argument,' interjected Charlie. 'I wondered how long it would be before you got round to that Russian political despot.'

Terry sighed, then said, 'You birdbrained nincompoop, people like you are a menace to working-class society. For your personal edification, Karl Marx was a socialist philosopher, born of Jewish descent in Germany. He abandoned philosophy for social economy, and because of his zeal in pursuing his theory of "shared wealth" he was driven out of Germany, France and Belgium by the powers that be who wished to retain the status quo of wealth supported by poverty. He finally settled in England where he spent a good deal of his time reading the works of other economic theorists, such as the Parisian physiocrats.'

'Parisian physiocrats?' exclaimed Sandy. 'Who on God's

earth were they?'

They were a school of eighteenth-century French economists, who were named after "physiocracy", the name given by Dupont de Nemours to the economic doctrines of Quesway, formulated in about 1750 in his articles that were published in Diderot's *Encyclopaedia*,' Terry replied.

'What was he beefing about, this Dupont de Nemours?' Charlie sneered, 'I suppose he was another bloody communist, wasn't he?'

'No! He wasn't a bloody communist as you so succinctly put it. He was a French intellectual with a special interest in economic theory. He thought there were natural economic laws that should not be transgressed, and that governments should follow a policy of laissez faire or laissez passer.'

'What does that mean, Terry? Brains asked.

'The non-interference with natural economic laws. His hypothesis was that land was the ultimate source of all wealth, and that trade and industry simply transformed its products.'

'What's all that got to do with Karl Marx?' said Sandy.

'Well it should be obvious even to you lot of politically subjugated, propaganda blighted, under educated, untutored lot of miserable sods that other economic theorists borrowed or refined many of the ideas that had fermented in the brains of the French physiocrats. Of course they are people whose names you have never heard of, for example Boisguibert and Vauban, and British economists such as John Locke, David Hume and Adam Smith.'

'But there were other economists with theories of their own, weren't there, Terry?' Old Joe said.

'Of course there were. For example David Ricardo, who like Karl Marx came from a Jewish family. He wrote papers on economics from a political standpoint and was the first to elucidate clearly on the Quantity Theory of Money.'

'What does that mean?' said Sandy.

'In a nutshell it means the value of money is in its scarcity; or in other words the more money that's in circulation the less value it has against its purchasing power. In simple terms it's called inflation, which is too much money chasing too few goods and services. Then there was the Reverend Thomas Malthus who theorised in an essay called "The Principles of Population" that populations tend to increase faster than the means of subsistence, and that their growth can only be checked by moral restraints or by disease or war.'

'Where does Karl Marx come into all this?' said Charlie.

'Well now, that's the interesting point in this debate. You see Karl Marx spent most of his free time in the reading room at the British Museum, studying the works of earlier and contemporary economists. What he did, together with his friend Friedrich Engels, was to refine and redefine their hypotheses into a logical argument as it related to wealth, wages and poverty. Between them they came up with the economic theory that, broadly speaking, the repression of wages paid to the wealth-creating working population increased misery and intensified the class conflict, as expressed by Engels' *Condition of the British Working Classes* in 1844 and *The Communist Manifesto* of 1848, which talked about "the intensification of the exploitation of labour, and the monopolistic ownership of the instruments of production that would enable the capitalist classes to appropriate the economic benefits of the growing socialisation of the labour process, which merged the product of the individual worker into a social product in which his share could not be identified".'

'What the hell does all that jargon mean?' said a bemused Charlie. 'It's just like those bloody communists to give us a load of gibberish we can't understand.'

'Yes, a bit like the Mass in your church—all in Latin,' Albert remarked.

'Pack it up, you two,' Old Joe interjected. 'Let Terry get on with his patter, or we'll never get to know how we became wage slaves.'

'Well, then,' continued Terry, 'after much research Karl Marx came to believe in a "subsistence theory of wages", which meant the wealth-earning labouring and artisan classes were kept down to a level that ensured a certain necessary level of reproduction, whereas the "surplus value" of increasing productivity accrued to the landlords (who controlled rents) and the capitalists (who controlled production) – who in Karl Marx's opinion were merging into one exploiting class.'

'What does all that mean, Terry?' said Brains, 'I couldn't follow all of it.'

'Simply, my old friend, that the owners of land who controlled rents, and the entrepreneurs who controlled the means of production, and the wholesalers and retailers who controlled the price of manufactured goods, between them had full control of the wealth-producing working classes, whom they kept in subjugation by the simple means of suppressive laws, passed by a parliament beholden to and controlled by them, as well as through low wages and a surplus pool of labour.'

'So what did Marx and Engels have to say on that score?' said Old Joe.

'To be blunt about it, they said the wicked bastard landowners, entrepreneurial factory, mines and mill owners, and others of their ilk, whose wives liked to be referred to as polite society, but who were in fact vindictive and cruel employers, were exploiting the labour markets through these low wages and surplus labour.'

'Surplus labour that came from where?' Albert asked.

'Mainly from peasants who drifted in from English rural villages, where land enclosures had caused destitution on an unimaginable scale. Many also came from Ireland where absentee landlords exacted high rents that caused abject poverty among the indigenous Irish rural population, but more especially after the potato famine of 1847–48, when thousands of Irish people died, and several million were forced to emigrate to England and America. Also there was a wave of migrants from the continent of Europe.'

'What else did Marx and Engels have to say on wage theory?' said Sandy.

'More or less what I've already told you. To economists wages and salaries are simply a way of maintaining the equilibrium, in other words the balance, between demand and supply, in this case the services of labour. However, since the demand for a particular sort of labour in a particular place may be liable to frequent fluctuations, as was the case during the period of the bubonic plague, so it will often happen that perfect equalisation between demand and supply involves frequent and large fluctuations in wages and salaries. Such fluctuations are intolerable to the wage earner, and actually diminish his efficiency as a worker. No wage system, therefore, has ever secured, or even aimed at securing, perfect equalisation. But that's enough on that subject.'

'I've got a question, Terry,' I ventured to say.

'What may that be, H?'

'It's your point earlier about manhood suffrage. I notice there was no mention of womanhood suffrage.'

'Yes! You're quite right on that score,' he replied, 'and in my opinion that was a grievous error on the Chartists' part, because, had womanhood suffrage been included in their Charter, you can bet that the politically frustrated upper class women of the day, whose feminist daughters later in the nineteenth century formed the suffragette movement, and suffered grievously for their cause, would have backed Chartism, and the political battle for universal enfranchisement would have been achieved, with or without bloodshed, long before it finally was.'

'Are you saying that the Chartists failed to advance political reform?' Albert asked.

'Not at all,' Terry replied. 'It was a bit like the parable of the sower of seeds, if you can recall those texts we used to get from Sunday school in our childhood.'

'What's a parable, Terry? said Brains.

It's an allegorical method of conveying instruction by means of a fable from which a moral is drawn, and before you ask what a fable is . . .'

'I know what a fable is! I've read Æsop's Fables, I have,' said Brains, with a self-satisfied smirk on his face.

'Then you must have read your Sunday school texts,' Terry continued, 'for as I was saying, I remember one text in particular in which Jesus tells us about a farmer who went out to sow seeds. Some fell by the wayside, and were trampled on and the birds of the air came and ate them up. Some seeds fell on rocks and when they came up the plants withered because they had no moisture. Other seeds fell among thorns, which grew up and choked the plants, but other seeds fell on good soil. They grew up and yielded a crop a hundred times more than was sown. Jesus said, "He who has ears to hear, then let him hear," or words to that effect. By the way, Charlie, that comes from Luke 8:25, just in case you want to know.'

'What does all that mean, Terry,' said Charlie, 'coming from a communist atheist like you?'

'Well, what it means in the case of Chartism is that the seeds for political reform had been sown, even though some of the seeds for reform had fallen onto thickheads and numbskulls like you. But against all the odds some seeds of political wisdom fell on the heads of uneducated but intelligent people. They began to germinate and, in spite of the apparent failure of the Chartists, a new generation of self-tutored political protagonists began to demand more democratic government. The seeds that had been sown by the Chartists spread their roots till finally in 1867 the House of Commons passed a Reform Bill, which doubled the number of eligible voters.'

'Did that include women?' said Albert.

'Of course not – nor did it include most men. The right to vote focused on how much rent was paid – ten pounds and over gave you the right to vote, if you were a man.'

'Was this the only country where citizens were disenfranchised, or was it general?' Duffy asked.

'It was mainly in this country, because manhood suffrage was already common on the European continent. That's possibly why in 1884 the Liberal party, under the premiership of Gladstone, succeeded in passing a bill that doubled the number of people eligible to vote. Of course you will have noticed that the labouring classes were still outside the remit of the franchise, as were women.'

'Why do you think that was, Terry?' said Charlie.

'Christ, mate!' exclaimed Old Joe. 'That should be obvious even to a devout God-fearing Christian like yourself. The lot that were wealthy had a vested interest in creating, then voting for the Tory party. They took over the public schools and turned them into fee-paying schools for the sons of the wealthy. You all know the schools I mean: Eton, Harrow, Rugby, Winchester and Marlborough – and the universities too. It was the party that wanted and still wants no change in social policy or the rigid class structure they had put in place, so they can continue to exploit the means of wealth creation – the labouring classes. The Liberal party knew they could rely on the votes of the artisan. That's why they extended the franchise to them, so as to include them in the voting system and give themselves a better chance of being elected or re-elected.'

'Well! I'm surprised, Joe,' said Terry. 'Where did you learn all that?'

'It was a major talking point when I was a kid. Getting close to civil war at times it was, especially in 1911 when Churchill was thinking of calling out troops against the dockers in London. It was Lloyd George who put a stop to that escapade, and that was only because he knew a war was brewing with Germany. He played on the dockers' patriotism to bring the dock strike to an end.'

'What has all this political claptrap got to do with slaves, serfs and wage slaves?' said Charlie.

'You tell him, Joe,' said Terry.

'Where shall I start?'

'Start with the build-up of the trade unions and the union movement, the catalyst that set fire to the archaic and corrupt political system.'

'I don't know what I can really say about trade unions,' said Old Joe, 'except that they grew out of the old trade associations of craftsmen that had existed in previous centuries. In the mid-nineteenth century trade union movements began to take off, from a slow start. Leaders such as Ben Tillett, who set up the Tea Operatives and General Labourers Union, Tom Mann, and Will Thorne, a semi-literate leader of the Gas Workers Union, who together with John Burns and many others began to forge alliances of workers. Then there were the socialist intellectuals who created the Fabian Society, which was set up in 1884, aiming to reorganise society by the emancipation of land and industrial capital from individual and class ownership, and vesting them in the community for the benefit of all citizens. The Fabians were named after Fabius Cunctator, the Roman general who defeated Hannibal, the Carthaginian general, by wearing down tactics rather than by the direct frontal attack methods usually employed in battle by the Roman legions.'

'Who were the Fabians?' Brains asked.

'The Fabian Society was founded in 1884 as a Socialist organisation. Among its illustrious founder members were Sidney Webb and Beatrice Webb, George Bernard Shaw and H.G. Wells, both of whom were great creative writers, and Annie Besant, who was a Fabian journalist and an advocate of birth control – but I'll come back to our Annie because of her trade union escapades later. So you see, those are the type of people on whom the seeds of Chartism fell, caused I suggest by the military suppression of that legitimate political movement, and out of whose brains the changes in social policies sprouted. That's about as much as I can tell you from what I know.'

'There you are. We have at least one member of the gang with some knowledge and intelligence, and in case you don't know it, Joe left school when he was twelve years of age, didn't you Joe?' said Terry.

'No! I left school in 1899 at the age of ten and started work in a leather tanning factory in London's East End.'

'Ha! Ha! Ha!' said Charlie, 'I'd have thought you'd had enough tanning at school to last you all the rest of your life.'

'Ignore that semi-literate imbecile, Joe,' said Sandy.

'Unfortunately, Sandy, we can't afford to ignore that form of ignorance,' Terry said, 'because it comes from a biased educational system designed to exclude the socio-economic policies that were inflicted on our forebears. But don't misunderstand me, education is the key to all human advancement, and no one knew this better than Prince Albert, the son of the Duke of Saxe-Coburg-Gotha, who was Queen Victoria's husband and consort till his death in 1861 from typhoid fever.'

'What did he have to do with it?' said Duffy.

'Well, it was mainly through his efforts that a royal commission was set up under Henry Pelham- Clinton, the 5th Duke of Newcastle, to look into the possible introduction of a national education policy.'

'He must have had a good reason for that,' said Albert.

'A damn good reason,' replied Terry. 'It was because he

realised the Japanese, French and Americans were beginning to produce manufactured goods which were beginning to infiltrate into what had previously been British overseas markets, and they had done this by implementing improvements in their education, which led to technological advancements, new inventions, improvements in the quality of their products and increased production.'

'So what happened after the Duke of Newcastle's royal commission had made its recommendations?' said Old Joe.

'The government of the day, under William E. Foster, began to work out a policy for the introduction of an education system. Don't misunderstand the situation, though. Some factory owners, men such as Robert Owen, had known the value of education and had operated schemes on their premises since the end of the eighteenth and the beginning of the nineteenth centuries, as I've already told you. An education act known as the Foster Act was passed by parliament in 1870. The act's proper designation was the Elementary Education Bill, and it introduced compulsory education for all children between the ages of five and ten.'

'Yes, that's the lot I came in,' said Old Joe. 'I left school when I was ten.'

'What year was that, Joe?' said Duffy.

'I've already told you,' Old Joe replied. '1899, that's the year that I started work, that was.'

'Never mind all that old patter. What happened next, Terry?' said Sandy.

'The next two acts to be passed were the Balfour Act of 1902 and the Fisher Act of 1918: that was the act that raised the school leaving age to fourteen, and the act we were educated under because we all left school before the war, didn't we?'

'Not quite,' I replied. 'I left school in 1944.'

It was then that Charlie our ship worker called down the hold, 'George, the fog's clearing and the dunnage lorries are on the quay. Get the lorries discharged before you go to "Beer Ho". You'll have to put the dunnage on the quay till you've uncovered the deck hatchway.' Then his voice trailed away as he made his way towards the other hatches, to give the other down-hold foreman his instructions.

'Where in hell has George got to?' exclaimed Charlie. 'What shall we do, Terry?'

I was already making my way to the Stothart and Pitt quay crane, climbing up through the deck booby hatch, when I heard Terry say, 'Brains, you go to the galley and make the tea. Pitch hands, you can go ashore and reeve wires round the dunnage ready for Henry to lift the sets off the lorries onto the quay. The rest of us had better get up on deck and strip off the tarpaulins and hatch covers, ready for Henry to remove the ship's hatch beams. We'll get the dunnage aboard as soon as the hatches and beams are cleared, have our tea, and then we can lay the dunnage out while we're waiting for the London quay gang to turn up. What's the time now?'

'It's a quarter past ten,' replied George, who had miraculously appeared from nowhere like a fairy godmother in a stage pantomime, 'so let's all get a move on or we won't be ready to start loading general cargo off the quay, that's if or when the Londoners get here.'

By the time we had finished our chores the dunnage lorries had been discharged and had driven off, the deck hatches and beams had been removed, and the dunnage timber put aboard the ship for the down-holders to lay over the cement cargo, ready for over-stowing the bagged cement dust with general cargo from the transit shed. Brains had returned from the galley by the time we had finished our chores, and, like the end of all good children's nursery stories, we all gathered together in the upper 'tween deck, where we all sat down on the warm bags of cement, along a table made up of planks of sweet smelling apple wood dunnage, to have our tea.

7

Abraham Lincoln

We had finished our tea break by 10.15 a.m. But instead of going up into my crane cabin eyrie I chose to stay in the 'tween deck to help the down-holders lay dunnage over the cement cargo. This was so they would be ready, when the London quay gang arrived, for the Londoners to begin wheelbarrowing general cargo out of the transit shed onto loading boards sited between the crane track on the quay.

We knew from our own experiences of travelling in the dilapidated, war-weary railway carriages and other rolling stock in use on the Fenchurch Street to Southend Railway that the London dockers or stevedores who had been allocated to work as our ship's side gang wouldn't be with us till at least 11 a.m. if they were lucky. This was because, even when they finally arrived at Tilbury Town railway station via Plaistow and Barking stations, they had first to report to the Port Authority Labour Master's office at the northern end of Tilbury Docks; then they had a walk of some half a mile from the Labour Master's office to the Southern Docks office, from where they would be directed to report to the Port Authority's shed foreman's office in the transit shed for orders.

Once they had been 'told off' in gangs and received their orders, the men then had to secure for themselves hand-propelled wheelbarrows from the stock assembled in the transit shed's appliance area, after which they then invariably had to wait for a second OST clerk (the stick-man – an OST clerk or docker whose job it was to measure all cargo to the nearest inch, and call out all marks and numbers to be recorded by the OST clerk who was already attached to the ship's gang) to arrive. Believe you me, Gilbert and Sullivan could never have produced a more pathetic, time-consuming or costly comic opera than that enshrined in the transfer of labour between docks or other ports – a process brought about by the Dock Workers (Regulation) of Employment Act, the regulations of which were controlled by the National Dock Labour Board through their respective Local Dock Labour Boards.

However, having exhausted my diatribe on the waste of time and money as it related to labour allocation within the port transport industry, I have to tell you that preparing a ship ready to receive cargo in a ship's hold always reminded me of King Henry V's speech in Shakespeare's play: 'Once more into the breach, dear friends, once more, or close the wall up with our English dead.' But as Terry pointed out, 'We don't require a speech to urge us on, even though we've often found ourselves "in the breach", so to speak, during our wartime experiences. Now we are wealth creators, being manipulated by one of the major elements of a capitalist-controlled eco-social system – money. So we toil as wage slaves under the piecework rate payment system in order to live, and will do so till we retire, if we're lucky enough to live, or till we die.'

We had finished laying the dunnage by 10.45 a.m. and were surprised when Charlie, our ship worker, put his head over the open hatchway to announce, 'The quay gang's arrived and there are sets of cargo on the quay, chop-chop.'

George looked at his watch. 'Christ!' he said, 'They made good time. Let's get to it then.' So without any prompting each one of us went to our action station, me up into the crane cabin to concentrate on the job on hand, and my workmates to prepare for the sweating toil of putting together the giant jigsaw puzzle that stowing cargo into a ship's hold really was. It was an exercise that was about to proceed as George made his way ashore to select the puzzle pieces from the general cargo in the transit shed that was awaiting shipment.

The freight we were about to put aboard the ship was bound for Dubouti, a port at the far eastern end of the Red Sea, the first port of call for the ship on her outward voyage. The cargo was destined for other ports down the East African coast, and would be transshipped by short sea traders or Arab-manned and -owned dhows or coasters once it had been discharged.

When they started work the London quay gang really put their backs into the job, and I was kept busy hoisting sets of cargo into the hold till lunchtime at noon, when one of the pitch hands called up to Old Joe that the quay gang had 'knocked off' and I began to climb down the three vertical steel ladders of the crane's superstructure just as Terry's head emerged through the ship's booby hatch.

Terry and the rest of the gang clambered down the ship's gangway, followed by Old Joe swinging his two dud legs like pendulums. We all met on the quay and walked to the bottom canteen, where we went through the same old procedure of getting served with a sandwich or roll, a mug of tea or a glass of beer. Then, on finding an empty table with benches, we sat for some time in silence while we ate and drank. Then Brains said, 'You got up as far as telling us about the Balfour Education Act and the Fisher Education Act, Terry.'

'Oh, yes!' said Terry, brought back to reality with a start, and returning to where he had left off with his lecture on slavery, serfdom and wage slavery as though there had been no interruption. 'But,' he said, 'there was a far more important Act passed in 1936. It was an Education Bill set to raise the school leaving age to fifteen years for some children, but it also allowed for exemptions so other children could leave school aged fourteen, if their parents could satisfy the local education authority that beneficial employment was on offer. There was strong opposition to the exemption clauses from local authorities, teaching bodies and working-class educational and industrial organisations, but Stanley Baldwin's government refused to withdraw the obnoxious clauses and both the House of Commons and the

House of Lords passed the Bill. But the seeds for the future advancement of education had been sown in the previous century. There was to be no turning back of the clock, although it was not till the 1944 Education Act (known as the Butler Act) was passed by Winston Churchill's wartime coalition government that the exemption clauses in the 1936 Act were reversed. But I'm jumping the gun here because there were two more important issues that have to be addressed.'

'What are they?' Sandy asked.

'The first obvious one, and the most important one that you all seem to have forgotten, is slavery.'

'We thought you had finished with that topic,' said Duffy.

'Not quite,' replied Terry, 'because well into the nineteenth century slave traders were still shipping slaves into the southern American states, to work on the cotton and sugar plantations and to act as lackeys and scullions doing household and other menial chores for plantation owners, even though in 1833 the British government had passed an Act which liberated thousands of slaves in the British West Indies.'

'How did the Americans react to that?' asked Albert.

'I think that might have been one of the sparks that ignited the American War of 1861–65.'

'One of the sparks?' Duffy interrupted. 'Was there another one?'

'I think there was,' said Terry.

'What was the other one?' said Old Joe.

'White immigration,' replied Terry. 'You see, after the potato famine in Ireland, and the upheavals caused by wars in Europe, hundreds of thousands of European citizens fled to America. Now the population of the northern states was hardly going to turn white immigrants into slaves, at least not once wage slavery had been discovered to be far more income-producing than shackled slaves, and no doubt having seen what had happened in the British West Indies with the abolition of slavery, the American President, Abraham Lincoln, sought its abolition in America.'

'Why did he want to do that?' said Duffy. 'After all,

hadn't slavery become endemic in the American southern states?'

'Yes it had, like foot and mouth disease in some cattle is endemic, but Lincoln had always been against slavery. You see, Lincoln was what Americans called a "backwoodsman", or what we might call a "country bumpkin". He had had experience of physical hard labour himself, and the subjugation of both body and mind that ignorance imposes on ordinary people. He was born in 1809 and had a very minimal education, just like you lot, but he rose through various occupations to become a lawyer – which is interesting in so far as London waif, stray and foundling children who had been left in the undercroft at Lincoln's Inn Fields, where the legal-beavers have their chambers, and who were invariably shipped off to America, were all named Lincoln. So, although Abraham Lincoln was known to have been born in Kentucky, his father or grandfather may have been a London-born foundling. Lincoln then entered Congress to represent Illinois in 1846. In fact, Lincoln was one of the leaders of the Republican party, which had been formed in 1856 to oppose slavery.'

'That was a dangerous thing to do in America those days, wasn't it?' said Old Joe. 'After all, although I don't know much about American history, I do know the southern states had become rich by imported slave labour from Africa, slaves who worked in the cotton and sugar plantations!'

'Yes, Joe, of course you're right, but as I've been explaining to you, slave labour had taken on a new dimension together with a new name, wage earner. However, it was Lincoln and fellow members of the Republican party who are purported to have begun the debate on anti-slavery in America in 1856, and it is said that this brought him back into politics, together with Stephen Douglas, a co-conspirator in the eyes of the Confederate southern states. Lincoln was elected President in 1861, and it was in that year the Confederate states proposed to withdraw from the Union; and war broke out between them.'

'Wasn't it a civil war, Terry?' I asked.

'That depends how you look at the structure of American government. Is America a single nation, or is it a number of separate nation states with their own governments that are federated by a controlling legislature?'

'Well, is it, Terry?' Duffy exclaimed. 'What does that mean?'

'In simple terms it means they are nation states that have banded together in league for some common objective, with a government that is made up of representatives from each of the states within the union. So, my answer to your question is that the conflict that raged between the northern and southern states was not a civil war but a war between nation states, a war that was won by the Union government under Abraham Lincoln.'

'So that put an end to slavery in America, did it, Terry?'

'Slave labour, yes. It was on New Year's Day 1863 that Lincoln proclaimed the emancipation of Negroes. He was re-elected president in 1864, but shortly after his second inauguration he was assassinated by John Wilkes Booth, an actor, in 1865.'

'Well!' said Charlie. 'That only goes to show that not only can't you fool all the people all the time but you obviously can't please all the people all the time, either.'

'That must be a first for you, Charlie,' said Duffy. 'You got it right for a change. But I bet Booth was more of a comedian than an actor. Comedians are like politicians: you hear them constantly talking about work, but you never see or hear of them doing any. That's quite possibly why Booth assassinated Abraham Lincoln. He'd heard Lincoln had actually done some physical, useful work in his life and didn't want it to be generally known among the working population.'

'OK. That's enough on the subject of anti-slavery in America,' said Terry. 'Now I must return to the nineteenth century and the British trade unions' role in wresting some of the riches created by the wealth-producing classes away from their flagrant abusers.'

'How did the unions manage that?' said Sandy.

'Well, after the repeal of the Anti-Combination Laws in 1824, laws which forbade the existence of trade societies of any description for industrial workers, more especially at that time artisans and tradesmen, groups of workers began to band together to form trade and general workers unions of their own. In 1850 the Amalgamated Society of Engineers was founded, and in 1868 the Trades Union Congress was established. In 1871 trade unions were given full legal status and their funds some measure of protection, but picketing was still held to be illegal.'

'You lot will be held illegal if you don't get back on the ship. Look at the soddin' time!' we heard George call out through an open window. 'It's one o'clock and the quay gang have already started making up sets of cargo.'

We didn't even bother to look at our watches, but made a scramble for the canteen door, with me in the vanguard because I had the furthest distance to go to get up into the crane cabin before the down-holders got into the upper 'tween deck and the pitch hands arrived on the quay beneath the crane. I was installed in my crane cabin before Old Joe, bringing up the rear, puffed and panted his way up the ship's gangway onto the deck. I then looked at my watch. It read one o'clock. George had pulled another fast one on us on his way to being elevated to the pinnacle of his career and ambition, to be made up to a ship worker. I'd never seen a man change so much in such a short time – from being one of the lads to a monthly salaried slave driver. However, he wasn't in the exalted rank of regimental sergeant major in the army now, passing on orders to men who couldn't answer him back. For my part I was interested to know how he would deal with men when he was picking up gangs in the Dock Labour Board Compound, to work ships on his own account—Terry for instance. . . .

We (or to be honest the quay and ship's gangs) worked like beavers all the afternoon, stopping just long enough at 2.30 p.m. for a quick tea break, then continuing till just after 6.15 p.m. On our having finished working cargo off the quay, the Londoners, who were a gang of stevedores, were given their attendance books by the Port of London Authority shed foreman so they could get away to catch their train back home. However, by the time we had finished loading cargo off the quay all the space above the cement cargo up to the deck head had been filled. The only room left in the upper 'tween deck was the square of the hatch, and this coveted cargo space had been reserved for a barge-load of half round, brown paper-wrapped, tar-covered corrugated steel culvert plates, bound for Port Aden for transshipment to a Middle Eastern country. But that was work for tomorrow, so on the departure of the Londoners we replaced the ship's beams, hatches and tarpaulin covers before making our separate ways home. That is with the exception of Terry, Brains, Duffy, Albert, Sandy, Charlie and me, who made for Smokey Joe's café for what was meant to be a 'quick pint', but went on and on because of Terry's continued lecture.

*****

The drinking saga in Smokey Joe's café began when we asked Rosie for a pint each of Smokey Joe's best lukewarm urine-tasting Thames mouthwash. Rosie retorted by telling us that with the sort of foul language we used we needed all the mouthwash we could get, urine-tasting Thames or otherwise. The reply she received was that we had to use fowl language (cluck, cluck, cluck), otherwise she wouldn't know what we were talking about. Rosie, intent on having the last word, rolled her eyes at Terry and said, 'That doesn't include you, Terry darling. You talk lovely, you do. Not like the rest of them there, that common lot of uncouth krakens.'

'I think you mean cretins, Rosie,' Terry said. 'Krakens were mythical Norwegian sea monsters. Cretins in this case would mean stupid persons.'

'Well!' exclaimed Rosie. 'Fancy that, two for the price of one.'

Terry smiled but said nothing more. He simply walked over to the table where we had taken up residence and sat down. 'Do you think we've upset Rosie?' said Brains. But we sat sipping away at our glasses of beer, eyelids closed, with satisfied smiles on our sweat-stained faces, at peace with the world.

Rosie looked across at us, and her face broke into a smile as she said in a low voice to herself, 'The cheeky lot of sods.'

It was some minutes later that Duffy said, 'What more can you tell us about trade unions, and what difference have they made to the working classes, Terry?'

Terry, whose eyes had been diverted towards the bar counter by Rosie, who was leaning across the bar and winking at him, turned to look round the table before replying. Then he said, 'The first thing I can tell you about trade unions that may surprise you is that legally a trade union can be an association of either employers or workers, and a few employers' associations are actually registered as trade unions under British law. But the name is usually applied only to an association of wage earners – or salary earners – formed primarily for the purpose of collective action for the forwarding or defence of its professional interests.'

'What sort of interests are you referring to?' asked Albert.

'Mainly wages and conditions of employment, which are negotiated jointly. However, you must understand that most people among the general public think trade unions operate only in the interest of what employers and the media call "the labouring classes", but we know that's a lie for two reasons. The first is that by whatever name capitalists, the media or ignorant members of the other so-called upper social classes care to call us, we are members of the wealth-producing fraternity of workers, and second we also know that a growing number of "salary earners" have formed their own trade unions.'

'Why have they done that, Terry?' asked Sandy.

'For the same reason our grandfathers, grandmothers, fathers and mothers created the trade union movement,' said Terry. 'It's in order to negotiate terms and conditions of employment with their employers. But unlike our kith and kin of the wealth-producing classes, who fought for and shed blood to change the law in order to be allowed to set up trade unions, the salaried earners waited till after the law was changed before deciding on reflection that perhaps after all joint negotiation wasn't such a bad idea, and jumped on the bandwagon of trade unionism – simply in order to protect their own long term employment interests.'

'So are you saying most employed people belong to trade unions, Terry?' said Duffy.

'Yes, of course they do, even if their unions call

themselves the professional associations of this, that or the other, or the federation of this, that or the other: under the employment laws they are still trade unions. However, as I have previously explained, in Britain trade unions were entirely forbidden by law from 1799 to 1824 under the Combination Acts of 1799 and 1800, acts which remained on the statute books till 1824 when, through the persuasive efforts of Francis Place and Joseph Hume, there was a change in political attitudes which caused a Combination Repeal Act to be passed, followed in 1825 by government measures which gave trade unions a bare right to exist, but severely circumscribed their activities.'

'What does circumscribe mean, Terry?' said Brains.

'To hamper, restrict or curtail their activities.'

'So what followed that?' said Albert.

'Well, as I have already explained, Karl Marx and Friedrich Engels, both active propagandists of socialist theories, had put forward a communist manifesto.'

'What's a manifesto, Terry?' said Brains.

'It's a declaration of policy by a political party that it states it will carry out on behalf of the people if elected. To continue, it can be argued that it was the contents of the Marx-Engels communist manifesto that spawned a number of national "reformist socialist movements" in Europe, and in England where there had never been a properly constituted socialist party. The Social Democratic Federation, which had been founded by such followers of Marx and Engels as Henry Hyndman, a Cambridge-educated British writer and economist, and such non-Marxist sympathisers as William Morris, an Oxford graduate, poet, art-worker and the son of a wealthy merchant, and Belfort Bax, an English socialist writer who had studied in Germany, and later the Fabian Society, who as you will remember from our previous talks, was founded by Sidney and Beatrice Webb, George Bernard Shaw and other radical intellectuals, who attached their ideas more firmly to Ricardo's economic doctrine of rent than to the Marxist theory of surplus value.'

'Wasn't Ricardo's rent doctrine much the same as Marx's theory of surplus value?' Albert asked.

'More or less in my opinion,' replied Terry. 'The best way

to illustrate the difference between the two economic ideologies is to compare, for example, butter and margarine. Butter is made from animal fat via milk, while margarine is made mainly from vegetable oils, but both products tend to serve the same purpose. Butter is used mostly by the wealthy, whereas margarine is cheaper to buy and is therefore mostly used by the poor.'

'So what did all these economic theories and arguments lead to?' I asked.

'Among the intellectual classes, they fomented radical changes of opinions and political attitudes,' said Terry. 'The Fabians didn't believe revolution would solve the problem of social change, but that a gradual increase of state and municipal control over individual enterprise, and the already existing forms of social control, for example the civil service, local government and other public organisations, would gradually develop into a revolutionary collective control over the social and economic life of the nation.'

'Isn't that the same idea as Marx's communism?' said Albert.

'Yes and no!' exclaimed Terry. 'We're back to the difference between butter and margarine – but whatever it was, it couldn't be worse than the socio-economic misery of uncontrolled, unfettered, laissez-faire capitalism for the wealth producers of the nation, who lived among violent, antisocial neighbours, in slum dwellings controlled by heavy-handed landlords, in abject poverty where diseases ran riot, which, coupled with malnutrition, brought about infant mortality rates of prodigious proportions among the newly born and young.'

'It's still like that now in the East End,' said Duffy, 'It hasn't changed since I was a kid growing up there. My family lived in a rat-infested tenement block outside the West India Docks, just off Ming Street, before we got a council house in Tilbury.'

'Then you should consider yourself lucky,' said Terry. 'Think what it must have been like in the 1850s, before the advent of trade unions. But that's enough about that. Let's get back to the subject of trade unions proper. As we have already discussed some of the fore-runners of the trade union movement, let's go on to the front line fighters who took the battle for better wages and conditions of employment in mills, factories, docks and mines right into the capitalists' heartland in their struggle for a fairer deal.'

'Do you think the trade unions have achieved a fairer deal, Terry?' asked Sandy.

'Yes and no!' Terry exclaimed again. 'It depends how you look at the problem. What you have got to remember is that to bring about socio-economic change was always going to be an uphill struggle however it was undertaken. The Fabians knew from previous experiences, such as the Gordon Riots of 1780, the Peterloo Massacre of 1819 and later experiences during the 1870s and 1880s, mainly caused by trade depression, unemployment and poverty, that armed insurrection was not going to bring about socio-economic change in the short term. Like all theorists, the Fabians were looking to, and planning for, the long term, but like the poor bloody infantry in any battle, the half-starved, ragged trousered workers and their families were taking casualties – not through bullets or bayonets but through malnutrition, industrial and social diseases and increasing numbers of industrial accidents; and not only among male employees but among women also. Something drastic had to be done to stem the flow and turn the tide of what had become a national disgrace and a social disaster.'

'So what did turn the socio-economic tide, Terry?' said Brains.

'A lady by the name of Mrs Annie Besant, a Fabian journalist and birth-control advocate and propagandist, whose article 'White Slavery in London' in her paper, the *Link*, on 23 June 1888, first drew attention to the low pay and disgraceful, dangerous conditions in which match-making women, girls and children worked for Bryant and May in London's East End.'

'What happened?' asked Sandy.

'They did what no other group of workers had ever done. In 1888 they went on strike when Annie Besant's three main informants were sacked. There was no violence. It was a passive demonstration of worker solidarity, and it worked. Now it was the men's turn to take action for better working conditions and pay. So in 1889 the Great Dock Strike began.'

'There will be a few more strikes when you lot get home tonight. Your wives will be doing a bit of rolling pin striking as you go through the door. Look at the time!'

There was a sudden mad scamper for the rear door of Smokey Joe's café, as we made a dash for home. The last we heard as we dashed out through the doorway was Rosie's shrill voice calling after us, 'Goodnight, lads – good luck. You'll need it!'

8

The Australian Dockers

*T*he following morning at 8 a.m., when most of our ship's gang had arrived at the ship's side, Terry and the other debaters were absent, but they could be seen wending their way slowly down the half mile of quay towards us. George was waiting for us at the foot of the gangway. He was in his newly found ship worker type of authoritative but pensive mood, with arms folded across his chest, waiting to give us his orders. Well! They weren't really his orders. They came from the Loading Officer via Charlie the ship worker, but impression is almost as good as the genuine article if the recipient has no knowledge of the real thing. So there stood George, our down-hold foreman, who was soon to be elevated to the position of ship worker, pumped up like a puff adder but for a different reason, while he waited for the miscreant latecomers to arrive.

'You're soddin' late!' he said, with malice in his voice.

'Late we may be, but sodden we're not,' Terry replied. 'Well at least not till we get down into the ship's hold and start to sweat. Anyway, what's the problem?'

'There's been a change of plan. We're not loading the steel culverts that were originally down on the ship's loading plan; they're now going to number four hatch. We've got a lighter of oil drilling equipment for Aden; that's for transshipment to one of the oil-producing states in the

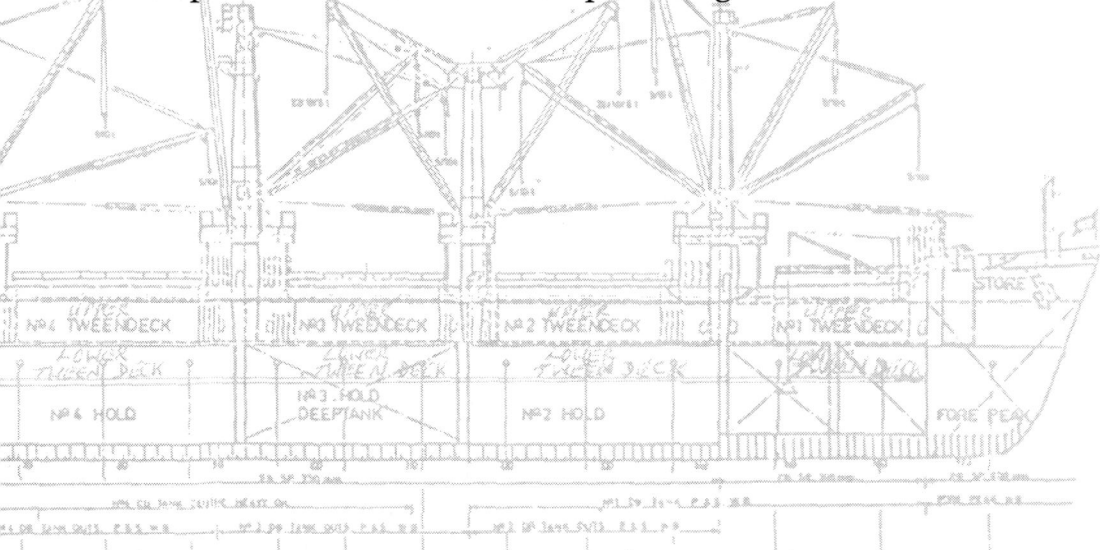

Persian Gulf. We'll be working over-side, so we'll need to get wires and dolly-bars from the stores. Henry, while the barge hands are getting the gear, get up in the crane and take the slab hatches and beams off, then bring the loading gear up onto the deck. The serang has had his lascar ship's deck crew break out the ten ton derricks and the lighter-man has uncovered the craft, so the sooner we get started the better.'

When George had finished giving out his orders, which were quite unnecessary as we were fully aware of our work functions, we stood where we were for fully a minute, before Terry said, 'Chop-chop you lot! Let's get to work! We're piece workers, don't you know. Time's money and George's promotion, too. Where do you think you are, in the House of Commons where you can sit on your arses all day, berating the wealth-producing classes for not working hard enough?' Then bleating 'Baa, baa, baa,' like a lost sheep, he led the men up the gangway onto the ship's deck.

George stood at the bottom of the gangway seething with rage as he watched the men follow Terry. He had purposely waited for the gang on the quayside, so as to be able to lead them aboard the ship himself. Now he was in spitting distance of becoming a ship worker, but Terry had unwittingly snatched the initiative from him. He wouldn't forget that slight, ever.

By the time the gang had removed the tarpaulin covers from the hatches, and I had taken the slab hatches and beams off the ship's hold and put the lifting wires and dolly-bars aboard the ship with the quay crane, a pro-rata winch driver had arrived from the Dock Labour Compound. He was a short, fat, bald-headed character, known to a good number of the older docking fraternity as 'Static', on account of his being excused from being sent 'out of sector' on labour allocation to London. This was because, so the story went, many years before, during the 1930s, when Static was working in one of the Upper Docks, it was said he'd grassed on his workmates. Londoners have long memories, so for his own safety Static was only ever employed in or about Sector 3, Tilbury Docks.

By the time I had come on deck the barge hands had clambered over the ship's side, made the perilous climb down a rope ladder into the waiting craft and had already reeved wires round the first bundle of oil drilling pipes, ready for Static and me to lift the set aboard ship. Old Joe was standing by the ship's rail with his hands held up to shoulder height, with fingers outstretched like an orchestra's conductor, about to set his musicians to make music. Only our instruments would make a much fiercer noise than any of the instruments in an orchestra, for our steam winches hissed and spat and gurgled and farted as they were first put into lower, then hoist positions, forward and reverse. The noise from a ship's steam winches was not unlike that of a railway shunting engine working in a marshalling yard – except it was continuous, as we first raised sets of pipes out of the craft, then lowered set after set of steel pipes into the upper 'tween deck. Then the nut and bolt fittings, which were also part of the consignment, were shipped and stowed between the lengths of drilling pipes.

We worked on all day except for two short morning and afternoon 'Beer Ho' times, when Brains made the tea and we all congregated in the upper 'tween deck. That is except for George, who had now taken to having his 'Beer Ho' break with the ship workers in their hut, and Static, who chose to go ashore to the PLA mobile canteen, knowing full well he had been sent to Coventry for life for his misdeeds of a quarter century before. His was a sentence based on the repugnance men felt for 'coppers' narks', men who had grassed up on their workmates to save their own skins, and 'blacklegs' too, who'd worked on during dock strikes. All were treated the same. The message of 'grass or blackleg' was passed on from father to son, stevedores and dockers, till the miscreants went out of the port transport industry forever.

It was just after 5 pm. that we completed the discharge of the lighter, but then we discovered there were two lorries on the quay with deck cargo. Static was paid off, the serang brought his deck crew out to put the derricks away, the barge hands went ashore to help the lorry drivers load their freight onto cargo boards, and I went back up into the quay crane to replace the ship's beams and slab hatches and put the deck cargo aboard the ship before knocking off time, when we all made our separate ways home. That is, except for those of us who went to Smokey Joe's café for a quick pint and a long discussion.

*****

As we entered Smokey Joe's, Sandy, who was in the lead, turned to us and said, 'Look who's in charge of the bar tonight. It's our Mary.'

Mary glared at us, turned her head to one side, put her nose up in the air, ran her hand along the side of her face, licked an index finger and wetted her eyebrows, then pertly said, 'What do you lot want?'

'Ah!' exclaimed Terry, 'It's our Mary, Mary, Mary who is so contrary, behind the bar for Joe, Now Mary, Mary, may I ask how does Joe's watered-down beer flow. Has it got bubbles and bile, that's come straight from the Nile, Where the pharaohs once bathed, and lived in great style. Or is it Thames water, the grist of the mill, The aqua non-pure that fills up Joe's till?'

'Oh! It's you, Mr Know-all, the dockers' QC. What are you going to lecher us on tonight?' said Mary.

'I think you mean lecture,' replied Terry, 'which is a discourse given before an audience on a given subject. Lecher means fornicator or debauchee.'

'My, my,' said Mary, 'aren't we a clever clogs.'

'Yes he bloody well is,' said Sandy. 'Now get on with your job and draw up seven pints of beer, or I'll come behind the bar and do the job myself.'

Mary grudgingly did as she was bid, making sure she served Terry last of all. He made his way to the nearest table where he sat and sipped at his pint of beer with his eyes closed for several minutes, as his body slowly relaxed to recuperate from the physical exertion of another day's hard labour. Then Brains said, 'You finished last time telling us about Annie Besant and the match girls' strike of 1888, then you began to tell us about the Great Dock Strike of 1889, Terry.'

'Ah! So I did,' said Terry. 'I can only give you a précised version of the events that led to the Great Dock Strike. The main leaders of the strike were Messrs Ben Tillett, John

Burns, Will Thorne and Tom Mann, H.H. Champion and Jas Toomey, aided by the ladies Mesdames Annie Besant, Eleanor Marx Aveling and Mrs John Burns. However, it has to be emphasised the strikers were not without sympathetic support outside the docking fraternity, nor for that matter from trade unions and others abroad. Among the foremost of these was Cardinal Manning, the Oxford educated, Roman Catholic Archbishop of Westminster, Catholic Primate of England, who it must be accepted had a vested interest as many of those on strike pay were Roman Catholics. But an even more interesting fact is that Cardinal Manning's intervention led to Pope Leo XIII's declaration in 1891 that trade unionism was a civilised and acceptable part of employment politics. Then there were the Australians, God bless them, who at a meeting in Brisbane held by the Wharf Labourers' Union, donated £150. By the time the strike had ended Australian dockers in Perth, Sidney, Melbourne, Brisbane and other sub-ports had raised over £30,000, which saved the day for the striking stevedores and dockers of the Port of London.'

'What were the main reasons for the strike, Terry?' said Charlie.

'In the main, they were pay and conditions of employment. We think we've got it bad today, with our four hour work turn and eleven work periods each week, with our six shillings for each time we prove attendance. But we are at least protected from fly-by-nights looking for a few hours' work to some extent by the Dock Workers (Regulation) of Employment Act, an Act that only permits registered dockers and stevedores to shape at the call stands or on the stones for work in the docks. In the days before, during and for many years after the Great Dock Strike, anyone could shape for work in the docks, and thousands of men did. All the strikers wanted from their employers was a fair day's pay for a fair day's work, and continuity of employment. All that employers wanted from the dockers was as much work as they could get done for as little money they need pay out, and this wasn't difficult when it was coupled with a vast pool of hungry men with starving wives and children, living in absolute squalor in rat-infested, disease-ridden slum dwellings outside the docks. That was the obvious general consensus of opinion among the ship owners and labour contractors who watched with psychopathic unconcern the plight of their fellow human beings. The horrible truth, however, about working conditions in the docks, the living conditions of dock workers' families, and the families of workers in other industries in Britain (with a few minor exceptions) were being highlighted by William Booth, founder of the Salvation Army, Dr T .J. Barnardo, founder of the children's charity, and Spencer Charrington, a member of the Charrington brewery family, who resigned his position at the brewery and became a staunch advocate of teetotalism. He was also made an honorary superintendent of Tower Hamlets Mission. Henry Mayhew was important too, a product of Westminster School whose social researches highlighted the dreadful working and living conditions of the underclasses of London, as was Henry H. Champion, editor of the *Labour Elector* during the strike.'

'But how did the strike start? What were the demands of the strikers?' Charlie asked, taking a keen interest now that the names of Cardinal Manning and the Pope himself had been mentioned.

'The initial dispute began,' continued Terry, 'over what was then termed "plus money", during the discharging of the *Lady Armstrong*, a sailing ship, in the West India Docks. "Plus money" was what we today call a "job and finish" payment based on the total amount of tonnage discharged. It appears that the East and West India Dock Companies had cut the "plus" bonus rates for the dockers, so as to attract ships into their own docking areas. In other words they were using the dockers' wage reduction to undercut their competitors in other dock companies during a trade depression. Apparently at that time there was an over supply of docking space and warehousing facilities. The cut in wage payments caused an immediate retaliation on the part of the dockers, and also provided the opportunity for long-held employment grievances to come to the surface.'

'So what were the men asking for?' asked Albert.

'That no man should be taken on for less than a four hour work period, contract and piecework to be abolished and wages to be raised to six pence an hour and eight pence an hour for overtime,' said Terry. 'However, the South Side Central Strike Committee had other ideas and issued a manifesto asking for different rates of pay for different categories of dock workers, which after all was only fair, taking into account the various types of work that had to be undertaken.'

'Did the strikers get what they asked for?' I questioned.

'More or less; but the point I'm trying to emphasise is that wage earners, so-called free men, were in a far worse position than bound slaves or serfs, simply because if they were unable to get work they and their families starved. At least slaves and serfs had to be housed, clothed and fed. But just as it seemed that the "wealth creators" were beginning to get the upper hand in their fight for socio-economic justice, a new evil appeared on the scene. They were the ultimate designs in wage slavery techniques.'

'What were they?' Brains asked.

'Time and motion studies,' said Terry.

'Who was responsible for introducing them?' Duffy asked.

'The time study technique was brought in by an American engineer, one Frederick Winslow Taylor, who had been apprenticed to a company called Sellers and Co. of Philadelphia. He later became the chief engineer of the Midvale Steel Company, but he is best known as the inventor of the modern system of what he called "The Principles of Scientific Management", which is now applied in most wage negotiation. In other words, what Taylor really did was introduce the system that is now called "vocational selection". This is designed to eliminate the unsuitable by means of his "differential piecework rates system", or what can only be described as the ultimate weapon in extracting from workers the maximum output for the minimum wage payment. It meant that those workers who couldn't stand the pace set by the employers, through their method study engineers, were classed as unemployable, and were sacked. In other words, as far as employers were concerned those former employees and their families could starve, and what's more, many did.'

'I don't suppose they use "vocational selection" work practices in Russia, Terry,' sneered Charlie, 'or do they?'

'Oh yes they do,' Terry replied, 'but in a different format and for a different reason. It was because the setting of production norms was a very important part of the Russian five year forward planning system. But you have to remember there is a big difference between Russian and Western political socio-economic ideologies: in Russia the output rates that are set for the "wealth-producing units", are set to maximise the use of each individual employed for the benefit of the community at large, and to maximise the number employed. In Britain and other European countries, as well as America, output rates are set to maximise the use of labour in employment, maximise output per unit of labour and minimise wage payments, while at the same time keeping a large pool of unemployed labour.'

'Rubbish,' Sandy blurted out. 'Workers wouldn't stand for it.'

Terry burst out laughing. 'What's so funny?' said Duffy.

'We already stand for it, all of us. As employees we don't have an option,' said Terry. 'For example, between us we've loaded 1,500 tons of cement into this ship paid at dead weight piece-work rates. That's not including the general cargo which is paid at measurement piecework rates. We shall all be paid off tomorrow night when we've finished loading the upper 'tween deck, and be sent back to the Dock Labour Compound to bustle and shove each other, trying to get another job. In twenty years' time do you think you'll be able to carry on doing this work aboard ships? Don't bother, I'll answer that for you. If you've not been injured, died from fatigue during one of our all day and night working sessions, or aren't suffering from some incurable disease such as asbestosis or farmer's lung contracted from handling cargoes, or haven't been injured or killed in a ship-board accident, you'll wind up pushing a wheelbarrow on the quay with the other old boys who've managed to survive till old age, till the day you die.'

'OK! You've made your point about the time study, Terry,' said Sandy. 'What about the motion study?'

'Oh! That was a work pattern system designed for laying

bricks by Frank B. Gilbreth. His method reduced the motions in laying a single brick from eighteen to five. That simple technique was said to increase the output from 120 bricks an hour to 350 an hour. This method of reducing motions in work operations was then experimented on in many other occupations and, when coupled with the timed movements designed by Frederick W. Taylor, hundreds of different jobs, mostly on assembly-line work but also covering a vast range of other occupations, were then included in what can only be described as the wage slave culture of paid employment. Under the new time and motion code that was introduced, wage rates were worked out that maximised output for the employer and minimised wages for the employee – but we've been through that exercise already, haven't we?'

'Yes we have, Terry,' said Sandy. 'And we all know how the upper crust live, with their big houses, posh cars and holidays abroad and such like. But what happened to all the real wealth that was created? Where did that all go?'

'You can tell them all about that tomorrow,' Mary called out. 'Haven't any of you lot got homes to go to? Just look at the time: it's 10.30 p.m.'

Terry looked up at the bar clock then yawned. 'Ah, so it is,' he said. 'I'll tell you on the morrow what happened to the real wealth that was accumulated through misery inflicted on the wealth producers over a couple of centuries.' Then, having finished his discourse, he rose slowly up onto his feet and, followed by the rest of us, made his way out of Smokey Joe's by means of the back door, and disappeared from view into the cold dank night air.

9

The Suffragettes

On the following morning, as each member of the ship's gang walked or rode their bicycles towards the loading ship, they could not but help noticing that she was flying her Blue Peter, a blue square flag with a white square in its centre, the captain's signal to both crew members and local traders who may be owed money for victuals and equipment that the ship was due to sail within the next twenty-four hours.

As each one of us arrived separately at the bottom of the ship's gangway we were surprised to notice George was not there, but had taken up station at the top of the gangway. It was obvious to all of the ship's gang that the reason for this move was to thwart any attempt to undermine his self-imposed authority before his real authority came into force on the commencement of his ship worker's promotion.

Terry was the last of us to arrive on the ship's deck. He'd come up the gangway bleary eyed to be met by George who said, 'And what time do you call this?'

Terry wasn't in a good mood after his late night session in Smokey Joe's. But he quickly retorted, 'Tell George the time, Brains, I think he's left his time-piece at home.'

'It's five past eight,' Brains innocently replied.

'Eight o'clock is your time to start work,' griped George.

'Is that right?' asked Terry. 'Then what are you all standing about here for? Let's get on with the job. What's on the work menu for today anyway? Come on, George, get on with it, what's our first job?'

George was flummoxed. He'd never been able to outwit Terry and now his regimented and disciplined mind was in turmoil till Terry gave him back the initiative. 'What's today's loading schedule, seeing as the ship's flying a Blue Peter?'

'Oh!' George replied. 'We've got a freight of cases of army stores and mail bags for Aden that are to be over-stowed on the oil drilling equipment.'

'Right,' said Terry, once again taking control of the gang. 'Come on you lot, let's get to work. Tarpaulins, hatches and beams off. George's got to go ashore and sort out the loading arrangements.'

George turned away and walked down the gangway seething with anger, closely followed by the pitch hands and me as we made our separate ways to our work stations, the pitch-hands to prepare the wires, ropes and cargo board for the loading operations, and me to climb up the three vertical steel ladders into the cabin of the Stothart and Pitt electric quay crane.

We very soon discovered we had no Port of London Authority quay gang, and the casework we were about to load was in fact army ordnance, that is anti-tank and tank gun barrels, rifles, sten-guns, revolvers and other such weaponry, which was contained in trucks and covered railway wagons. These were shoved along the quay railway tracks, under the quay cranes, by a Port of London shunting engine, and the pitch-hands revved the gun barrels in the wagons with wires for me to lift them aboard the ship. After completing that job they began to break out the sten-guns and rifles from the enclosed rail trucks. It was a slow, tedious job, made more so because we had Ministry of Defence personnel checking each case of the consignment before shipment. The military were being very security minded as British troops were involved in numerous skirmishes in Aden, where so-called terrorist organisations were demanding national independence.

The loading of the gun barrels didn't take more than an hour or so, but the cases of small arms were another story altogether, as each case was closely scrutinised for any sign of it having been tampered with before its arrival in the docks.

However, during the interminable periods between loading sets of cargo, Terry was able to continue the indoctrination of his workmates. 'Sandy asked me what had happened to all the real wealth that had been created. Where did it go? Well, the truth of the matter is that it went firstly on high living by the aristocracy and other land and property owners, entrepreneurs, wholesale merchants and, to a lesser extent, by retailing shopkeepers, university professors, the clergy, followed closely by the middle classes of the professions. In fact anyone of influence who wasn't employed in any way that was connected with the production of the wealth of the nation, all of whom kept themselves apart socially and physically from their proletarian, slum-dwelling, hungry, disease-ridden fellow countrymen, women and children.'

'But how did the upper crust go on getting away with it?' Duffy asked.

'Initially by the desperation of the poverty stricken masses to survive, but it was a situation that could not and would not be tolerated by them forever. We have already discussed the Peterloo Massacre of 1819, the Chartist movement of the 1830s and 1840s, and the Bloody Sunday rioting in 1887, which were mainly the inspiration of working-class leaders, as well as the Match Girls' Strike of 1888, and the Great Dock Strike of 1889 that was led by the trade unions with support from the Australians, and as importantly by the Catholic Church. We have discussed, too, the part played by Fabian Society intellectuals, who chose to work towards social and economic justice through parliamentary reforms instead of bloody revolution.'

'Yes,' said Duffy, 'but how did the non-producing upper classes go on getting away with the servitude they were imposing on the wealth producers.'

'Well, to be blunt about it, this phenomenon was mainly achieved and maintained by the upper classes conniving through secret societies, trade guilds or other means to subjugate their own race of people by the payment of low wages for long hours of work, dangerous conditions of employment, slum tenement housing conditions, meagre supplies of diseased water and inadequate sanitation.'

'But,' said Sandy, 'what happened to all the real wealth they had created?'

'It was spent on the building of an empire, through the subjugation of other nations, by the unopposed invasions of their lands, and on wars. Let's take just two wars as examples, the First and Second World Wars. The First World War is said to have cost the British government £7.8 billion, with 908,371 dead and some 10 million wounded. The Second World War is said to have cost the British government £28 billion, with over 400,000 dead and several million wounded, a figure that did not include people killed and injured while evacuated from their homes; but this did not include the war loans exacted from America.'

'Holy Mary,' Charlie burst out. 'What did that cost us?'

'Cost us is right, Charlie,' Terry replied, 'because it was the wealth-producing classes that not only fought and won the wars, but those who had survived it also had to work for the rest of their lives paying off loans made by America and Canada. In the case of the First World War it's on record that Britain's debt to the United States of America was £963 million, borrowed on behalf of the British government by Mr Stanley Baldwin, the Conservative government's Chancellor of the Exchequer. The loan was taken out in 1922. The Second World War's cost of £28 billion almost bankrupted the country, so on 6 December 1945 the Labour government under Clement Attlee was forced to borrow capital for the reconstruction of our industries and housing stock. America made two separate loans. These were the US Line of Credit, and Lend Lease, and amounted to $4.3 billion at two per cent interest, repayable over fifty years.'

'What about the Canadian loan, what did that cost us?' I asked.

'The Canadian loan,' said Terry, 'amounted in total to $1.2 billion, that's Canadian dollars of course, and is repayable over the same period at the same rate of interest.

It's reckoned that by the time these loans have been repaid they will have cost the British in excess of $10 billion.'

'Well, at the rate we're loading this hatch today that won't include us,' said Charlie. 'Why don't you go ashore, Terry, and see if you can get the job speeded up?'

Terry looked at his watch. 'It's lunchtime, let's go ashore,' he said. Then he called up to Old Joe on deck. 'Tell the pitch hands to close up the trucks and let the MOD blokes know we're going to lunch.' And with those last few words Terry made his way to the 'tween deck ladder, climbed it rapidly and disappeared through the deck bobby-hatch, quickly followed by the other gang members, and Old Joe who tick-tocked his way down the ship's gangway onto the quay, walking like a clockwork soldier about to go off parade. He was followed by the pitch-hands, then me, as we all made our way to the brewer's privately run bottom canteen, where we could sample the delights of whatever was on offer in the way of beer or tea, bread rolls or sandwiches.

We hadn't been sitting down for more than a few minutes, amid the comfort of the bottom canteen's wooden scrubbed tables and hard wooden backless benches, its cold tiled walls and flagstone flooring, when George, our erstwhile down-hold foreman, made a surprise appearance. We hadn't seen hide nor hair of him since he had gone ashore just after 8 a.m. that morning, so it was obvious to us that he was in practice for when he would be picking up gangs of men in his ship worker capacity. After all, you can't expect the captain of a ship to be seen mingling with the seamen: it's bad practice when trying to impose discipline.

Terry was sitting by a canteen window, reading his *Daily Worker* when George said, 'The ship's due to sail at nine o'clock tonight, so she can catch the ebbing tide on her way outward bound. The army's mailbags are not due to arrive on the quay till around seven o'clock. Are all of you prepared to work a "short night"?' (To explain, a short night meant working up till midnight.)

Terry spoke up for all of us. Without looking up from his newspaper he said, 'How many mail bags are there?'

'Two lorry loads,' replied George.

'That's about 500 mailbags; they'll do for beam fillings

when we've finished loading the rest of the casework. OK, George, we'll see you tonight when we've finished the job. We don't need you.'

George got up, but before he left he said, 'That should give you time to finish your tale on slaves, serfs and wage slavery, Terry. Isn't it time you left the docks and went into teaching or something? You're wasted working in here, you know.' George then walked briskly out of the canteen, and we didn't see him again till we had finished beaming and hatching the ship late that evening as we made her ready for sea, by which time it was almost nine o'clock.

Nothing more was said on the subject of slaves, serfs and wage slavery till the gang got back on board the ship. The job of loading the cases of small arms was as slow after lunch as it had been before. It seemed that the MOD were in no hurry to complete the job of clearing the railway wagons and getting the discharged trucks shunted off the quay ready for the Royal Mail lorries that were fetching the mail bags to arrive. So it was no surprise that during one of the long waiting period between sets Brains suddenly said, 'So how did slavery, serfdom and wage slavery come to an end, Terry?'

Terry stretched his arms, shook his head in disbelief and yawned.

'Brains, my old friend,' he said. 'Whatever gave you the impression that those suppressors of the human mind and body, inflicted by one group of human beings on another, have ever come to an end? The characteristics of slavery, serfdom and wage slavery are enshrined in the textbooks of the suppressors of human dignity, simply by their desire to benefit from the skills and labours of others. Those individuals limit the mental progress of vast numbers of humans to that of zombies, simply for personal profit or a lust for power. Those people have an evil side to their nature which, if it should ever come to an end, would give anyone who studies ethics a field day.'

'So what are you telling us?' exclaimed Albert. 'Slavery, serfdom and wage slavery still exist?'

'Yes, unfortunately slavery and serfdom are still endemic in some cultures, as is wage slavery in others,' replied Terry.

'However, I'm not prepared to get into a debate on the worldwide implications of slavery and serfdom, that's a job for the United Nations to undertake. The payment of wages is the next step up from serfdom, being paid to large groups of low, hourly paid workers. This is mostly women who are employed in non-unionised back street factories, more commonly known as sweat-shops, or as field workers on farms. As for wage slaves, that's us piece workers who have a low fixed basic wage, which is governed by the quantity of output we produce.'

'Yes, I understand all that,' said Duffy. 'But how and why did working conditions change so dramatically?'

'Well!' replied Terry, 'there are a number of reasons for that. First we have to thank the militant actions of our immediate forebears, those men and women who strived to create the trade unions that have obtained in many industries a fair day's pay for a fair day's work; negotiated agreements that have created better and safer working environments in many industries; organisations that have lobbied parliament in the pursuit of health and safety legislation in order to reduce industrial accidents and the incidence of industrial diseases; and who have obtained from some employers occupational pensions schemes. The second reason, and this is only because it came after the setting up of trade unions, but is in fact more important, is the setting up of the Independent Labour Party.'

'Oh!' exclaimed Charlie, 'I wondered how long it would take you to get round to bringing your neo-communist mates into your discussion.'

Terry laughed, then said, 'Do you know, Charlie, it's shallow-minded, semi-literate, semi-intelligent, numb-skulled cretins like you, who've been semi-educated mainly in church schools, by semi-trained religiously biased middle-class so-called teachers, who have held back social progress for the benefit of the wealth-producing classes since church schools first came into existence. But progress was made thanks to the foresight, the courage and the integrity of many literate, highly educated and intelligent individuals from the middle and upper classes, people who were thoroughly disgusted with the treatment meted out to the wealth-producing classes, who came together to form socialist groups in the eighteenth century. It was groups of radical free-thinking people such as the Social Democratic Federation and the Fabian Society who in 1893 collaborated with a self-educated Scotsman by the name of James Keir Hardie to set up the Independent Labour Party, whose elected parliamentary representatives were the first voices to be heard in the House of Commons that fully represented the wealth-producing classes. Democracy was at last slowly beginning to assert itself. Then, too, the suffragette movement (middle- and upper-class feminists who agitated in the latter half of the nineteenth and early twentieth centuries under the banners of the Women's Franchise League and the Women's Social and Political Union, and were not averse to resorting to militant methods when peaceful ones failed) was a movement similar to that of the match girls of Bryant and May's who had been led by Annie Besant but with a different objective – votes for women. The suffragettes partially achieved their aims of women's suffrage in 1918, when a certain group of women got the vote; then in 1928 all women over twenty-one years of age were finally given the franchise.'

'What's all this got to do with slavery, serfdom and wage slavery?' said Old Joe the hatchway-man, who now that the upper 'tween deck was almost up to the deck beam level was actually standing below the level at which the down-holders were working.

'It's a so-called democracy, Joe, not a true democracy. It's what is known as a parliamentary democracy based on the election of a single representative to vote on behalf of the constituents that elected him or her,' said Terry. 'But it has to be admitted that since ordinary men and women have had the right to vote, vast changes have been made in the socio-economic-political framework of this country. Slavery, however, was made illegal, as we have already discussed, in 1807. Serfdom has been all but eliminated, although it could be argued that groups of employees caught up in a company that's been taken over by another company are in the serf-employment category. Wages and salaries are now mostly negotiated between the major employers and unions, but wage slavery, piecework rates set by unscrupulous time and motion practitioners acting for the benefit of employers, has yet to be properly controlled to the benefit of both employers and employees.'

It was at this juncture that George graced us with his presence, 'It's 6 pm. and the pitch-hands are working on the last railway wagon,' he said. 'As soon as that truck's empty you lot can go to supper while the railway trucks and wagons are cleared off the quay. It's a bit unorthodox, but be back here at seven o'clock, by which time the Royal Mail lorries should have arrived.'

'We'll stay on board the ship, George,' said Terry. 'The bottom canteen's closed now, and there's nowhere else for us to go.' Then he turned to Brains, 'Go to the ship's galley and make a pot of tea.' As he left Terry called after him, 'If the chef's about, ask him if he's got any grub to spare.'

'OK,' said Brains. He took the gang's battered aluminium teapot from the equally battered tea-box and strode off towards the galley as fast as his legs would carry him. He soon returned with a pot of steaming tea and a bag of freshly baked cakes he'd scrounged from the lascar chef, for which he had paid him a shilling.

It was spot on eight o'clock when three army lorries (one more than we'd expected) arrived on the quay loaded with what looked like bags of mail, but which were obviously not. There were a few murmurs among the gang as to why the mail had not been delivered by Royal Mail vehicles, which was common practice. But we were on a job-and-finish short night, so the lads got stuck into the work, and before the ship was due to sail at 9 p.m. we had loaded the bags of army mail, stowing them between the ship's beams, replaced the ship's beams, the slab hatches and the tarpaulin hatch covers. The lascar deck crew had secured the hatch covers with their steel bars couplings and made them fast with steel wedges. I had lifted the secondary gangway off the ship and placed it between the rail tracks under the quay crane. The lascar deck crew had raised the ship's gangway mid-ship and secured it. The ship's derricks had been lowered and secured in their respective crutches. The dock pilot was aboard and the ship was now ready to sail.

Two Port of London tugs, the *Walbrook* and the *Lea*, had already attached towing wires to the ship's head and stern, and soon the steady beat of their propellers as they thrashed the dirty water of the dock began to gently ease the ship away from her berth towards the open lock gates. There, two Thames river tugs (*Arcadia* and *Hibernia*) were waiting to tow her out into the main stream of the river's fairway in Northfleet Hope. I thought that would be the last I saw of her, but as I was making the ferry crossing to Gravesend on my way home the ferry had to heave-to to let her pass on her way towards the estuary and the North Sea. She was, that P&O cargo ship, very soon just a silhouette, showing her black shadow ghostlike in the light of a silvery moon as she thrashed her way down Gravesend Reach, chased in the gathering darkness by a Trinity House pilot cutter that was ploughing through the phosphorescence of her wake. That really was the last I ever saw of her.

In the meantime, the gang members had made their own separate ways home. None of us had been able to inform our wives we would be working late, but in the docklands that was an accepted practice as there was no easy form of communication.

*****

Finally, and to bring this tale to an end, I have to tell you that with George's promotion to ship worker our ship's gang was split up. Sandy and I stayed with our regular ship worker, Charlie S, while the other gang members went over to work under George. Terry, on the other hand, left the docks and the last I heard of him was he had gone into the teaching profession. The obvious reason for this was that no matter whatever academic or professional qualification a docker held while he was employed within the port transport industry he was first and foremost a docker, and therefore there was no possible opening for him for promotion within the National Dock Labour Board, the Port Authority or with the port employers.

Nevertheless, Terry's fragmented teaching while I was employed in the loading of a P&O cargo ship, on the subject of slavery, serfdom and wage slavery, had a profound effect on me. Therefore the substance of his lectures will stay with me till my dying days. As too will the cause of the sufferings imposed on my wealth-creating forebears, who were forced to fight against the tyrannies imposed on them during their working lives. So too will their heroic struggles for democracy, and for their right to belong to a trade union. I will also never forget Terry's explanation of the formation of trade unions, and their right to exist and act on our behalf in wage and employment conditions negotiation. Thanks to Terry I now understand how it is that all free people have the right to elect members of parliament, and through their elected representatives choose the prime minister and government they want to represent them in the House of Commons.

Printed in the United Kingdom
by Lightning Source UK Ltd.
131236UK00001BA/7/P

9 781904 408376